THE PREACHING MOMENT

D0109685

Abingdon Preacher's Library

Liberation Preaching, Justo L. and Catherine G. González
The Person in the Pulpit, Willard F. Jabusch
The Preaching Moment, Charles L. Bartow
Designing the Sermon, James Earl Massey
The Preaching Tradition, DeWitte T. Holland
The Sermon as God's Word, Robert W. Duke
Creative Preaching, Elizabeth Achtemeier
The Word in Worship, William Skudlarek
Preaching as Communication, Myron R. Chartier
A Theology of Preaching, Richard Lischer
Preaching Biblically, William D. Thompson

THE PREACHING MOMENT

A Guide to Sermon Delivery

Charles L. Bartow

Abingdon Preacher's Library
William D. Thompson, Editor

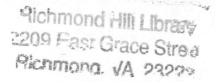
Richmond Hill Library
2209 East Grace Street
Richmond, VA 23223

ABINGDON
Nashville

0 2223

251
Bar

The Preaching Moment: A Guide to Sermon Delivery

Copyright © 1980 by Abingdon

Third Printing 1981

All rights reserved.
No part of this book may be reproduced in any manner
whatsoever without written permission of the publisher,
except brief quotations embodied in critical articles
or reviews. For information address Abingdon,
Nashville, Tennessee.

Library of Congress Cataloging in Publication Data

BARTOW, CHARLES L
   The preaching moment.
   (Abingdon preacher's library)
   Includes bibliographical references and index.
   1. Elocution. 2. Preaching. I. Title.
   PN44173.B3   251'.03   80-12370

ISBN 0-687-33907-3

Scripture quotations, unless otherwise noted, are from the Revised Standard Version
of the Bible, copyrighted 1946, 1952, © 1971, 1973 by the Division of Christian
Education of the National Council of the Churches of Christ in the U.S.A. and are
used by permission.

"Levitation" is reprinted from *Collected Poems 1951-1971* by A. R. Ammons, with
the permission of W. W. Norton & Company, Inc. Copyright © 1972 by A. R.
Ammons.

Lines from "After Apple-Picking," "Home Burial," "Birches," and "Pertinax" are
from *The Poetry of Robert Frost*, edited by Edward Connery Lathem. Copyright 1916,
1930, 1939, © 1969 by Holt, Rinehart & Winston. Copyright 1936, 1944, © 1958 by
Robert Frost. Copyright © 1964, 1967 by Lesley Frost Ballantine. Reprinted by
permission of Holt, Rinehart & Winston, Publishers. British rights granted by
Jonathan Cape Limited on behalf of the Estate of Robert Frost.

MANUFACTURED BY THE PARTHENON PRESS AT
NASHVILLE, TENNESSEE, UNITED STATES OF AMERICA

**To my wife—Paula
For her always affectionate
encouragement and support**

CONTENTS

EDITOR'S FOREWORD

Preaching has captured the attention of increasingly large segments of the American public. Lay parish committees seeking pastoral leadership consistently rank preaching as the most desirable pastoral skill. Seminary courses and clergy conferences on preaching attract participants in larger numbers than ever. Millions of viewers watch television preachers every week.

What is *good* preaching? is the question of both those who hear it and those who do it. Hearers answer that question instinctively, tuning in the preacher who meets their needs, whether in the pulpit of the neighborhood church or on a broadcast. Preachers need to answer more intentionally.

Time was that a good thick book on preaching would do it, or a miscellaneous smattering of thin ones. The time now seems ripe for a different kind of resource—a carefully conceived, tightly edited series of books whose scope covers the homiletical spectrum and whose individual volumes reveal the latest and best thinking about each specialty within the field of preaching. The volumes in the Abingdon Preacher's Library enable the preacher to understand preaching in its historical setting; to examine its biblical and theological underpinnings; to explore its spiritual, relational, and liturgical dimensions; and to develop insights into its craftsmanship.

Designed primarily for use in the seminary classroom, this series will also serve the practicing preacher whose background in homiletics is spotty or out-of-date, or whose preaching needs strengthening in some specific area.

William D. Thompson
Eastern Baptist Theological Seminary
Philadelphia, Pennsylvania

A WORD TO THE READER

As will become readily apparent to you in your reading of the following pages, this text is tightly constructed around the statement and explication of principles for sermon delivery educed from the discussion of the nature and purpose of preaching presented in chapter 1. In chapters 2 through 5, the principles are defined and explorations in the implementation of them are provided. In chapter 6, certain technical considerations in voice and articulation are discussed in light of those principles. Chapter 7 deals with the listening preacher's body talk, and in chapter 8, the principles of sermon delivery are interpreted and used as criteria for evaluation of preachers' efforts in specific preaching moments. The book may be used most profitably, therefore, if its format is followed—if chapter 1 is read first, and if the theoretical and exercise materials of the remaining chapters are used in order.

It also should be noted that this book is concerned with questions of substance, as well as of technique. In other words, no sharp dividing lines are drawn between content, form, and expression. It is my conviction, in fact, that drawing such lines not only is not helpful but is positively misleading. Frankly, without form there can be no perception of substance and hence no discernible content to any message; and without giving expression both to the form and to the substance of a matter, there can be no communication—no sharing of meaning; there cannot be even rational communication with one's self. In preaching, substance takes shape and finds expression in the preaching moment. *What* to preach and *how* to preach, therefore, are but two ways to put the same question. Like poetry, preaching "survives / In the valley of its saying . . . it survives, / A way of happening, a mouth."[1]

It also should be recognized that there are many issues of importance in homiletical theory, no more than hinted at in this text: theological issues concerning inspiration and authority in preaching; issues raised in consideration of preaching as a rhetorical, communications event; issues having to do with the relationship of preaching to other kinds of oral and written discourse; issues concerning preaching and the exercise of aesthetic judgment. It would have been great fun to kibitz a bit with regard to all of them. I have doggedly avoided the temptation to do so, however. In the notes, some direction is given those who may wish to "read up" or at least to start thinking more deeply about a few of these issues. But by and large, substantial attention is given only those matters that bear directly upon the question of sermon delivery—what it is and how it may be done.

I want to thank a number of people who directly or indirectly have contributed to the composition of this book: W. J. Beeners and William Brower, respectively professor and associate director of speech at Princeton Theological Seminary; Donald Macleod, professor of worship and preaching, also of Princeton; William D. Thompson, who invited me to write this text and who has so ably provided editorial comment and encouragement; students who have challenged and inspired me at Princeton Theological Seminary, New York Theological Seminary, and most recently, at The Lutheran Theological Seminary, Philadelphia; the members of The Presbyterian Church of Deep Run, who graciously have supported me throughout the months of preparation of the manuscript; Paula Largent, who typed chapter 1; and my wife Paula who, with diligence and love, typed all the remaining chapters. Whatever is best in *The Preaching Moment* is due to their contribution. Whatever is clumsy or erroneous is due to my own.

Charles L. Bartow
Bedminster, Pennsylvania

I. THE TALK NEVER IS ALL

In Robert Frost's dramatic poem "Home Burial," a grief-stricken wife bitterly complains to her husband, "Oh, you think the talk is all." The problem: Neither husband nor wife seems able to speak about the loss of their child so that the other can hear. Consequently, each mourns alone. Words fly between the two. But the words do not pass; they meet head on, as it were, in midair collision, walling off husband from wife, so that their pain cannot be shared. And not being able to hear each other, they finally cannot speak to each other. She makes her exit, he bellowing after her, "I'll follow and bring you back by force. I *will!*"[1] But there is no reply. That's the end of it. The poem is over. The talk is done; the hurt goes on.

On occasion, preachers fool themselves into thinking that the talk is all. The old chestnut, "Tell them what you're going to tell them; tell them; then tell them what you told them," unfortunately, without a blush, sometimes is accepted as gospel truth. Some preachers act on it, and they go on to convince themselves that their "much speaking" actually has accomplished something. In preaching, however, as in any other form of communication, you will discover that the talk never is all. The talk is only half, and it is the least important half. The other half, and the most important half, is listening.

Listening is the most important half of writing your sermon, or compiling notes for it, or even extemporaneously composing it; for obviously, you cannot possibly say anything that you have not at some time heard. As Harold Brack has pointed out in his article "The Listening Preacher," preaching can happen only after something has been said or done to the preacher.[2] Thoughts are comprehended, feelings felt, convictions are established first in you, the preacher; then comes the talk. And with talk so warranted and motivated, there comes, as well, at least some hope of something happening in those who attend to what you say. If, on the other hand, your text or situation, biblical or otherwise, has said nothing to you, done nothing to you, stirred in you no thoughts, feelings, or convictions worth the effort to express, then you literally must be at a loss for words. "You can't say 'nothing' well," W. J. Beeners has said. And that is the truth. First you must have something to say. Only then is it possible for you to say it.

In saying what is on your mind and heart, the things that you feel you must say, there is a problem, however, and the problem is this: How do you talk so that others can hear? How do you talk so that others can hear you listening? There is no easy answer to that question, for each one of us listens in a different manner. Our way of attending to what happens to us is always unique.[3] In the Frost poem mentioned just a few lines ago, for instance, the way the husband attended to his loss of an infant son was vastly different from the way the wife attended to hers. For him, it was a matter of burying the child with little more than a sigh of despair, and then going on with the rest of living; while for her, it was holding on, and on, and on. As she put it, the world quickly turns away from its dead and gets back to life and living people and things it understands, but "I won't have grief so . . . Oh, I won't, I won't!"

The wife could not hear her husband's listening—his way of grieving—and the husband could not hear hers. Yet Frost could hear both, couldn't he? And he could express what he heard so that others also could listen to both the husband and the wife. His words, as Heidegger might put it, brought into being a world real enough for people to enter, to believe in, and to be changed by.[4] How many sermons have you heard that have accomplished that? Not many? Well, that, at least in part, is the purpose of preaching. It is part of its purpose, if need be, even to give to "airy nothing a local habitation and a name."[5] Be concrete when you preach, H. H. Farmer has told us.[6] And speaking similarly, T. S. Eliot is supposed to have said that it is the purpose of literature to turn blood into ink. If that is true, and I believe it is, and if it further is true that sermons may be thought of as a specific type of literature, whether they actually are written out in full or not, then it is the purpose of speaking that sermonic literature to turn the ink back into blood. Speak into actuality what you have on your mind, what you hold in your heart! Evoke worlds of meaning that people can enter, believe in, and be changed by!

But once again, How? Well, among other things, certainly you have to know *what* you are listening for. And you are *not* listening for ideas—at least not ideas in the abstract, cut loose from what occasioned them and dissociated from your feelings about them. Rather, you are listening for ideas, facts, opinions, feelings, or whatever, that start somewhere and that are headed somewhere and that mean to have you go along with them—ideas that may whistle Stop! against the ordinary course of your thoughts and that switch them down unexpected paths; or facts that contradict or confirm your opinions and your convictions. In other words, when you are listening to a sermon, your own or that of someone else, you are listening with some expectation of being changed. When Jesus preached his parable of the good Samaritan (Luke 10:25-37), for instance, he did not intend to leave his principal listener just as he found him, did he? Quite the contrary, he rerouted his lawyer-interrogator's thinking altogether. Rather than defining "neighbor" in some traditional way, as the lawyer no doubt wished him to do, Jesus brought out the meaning of the term in a moving tale of neighborly, solicitous action. And rather than allowing the lawyer to rest content with that only, Jesus pushed on with an exaggerated insistence upon people being neighborly always, everywhere, and toward everyone in sight—an impossible task! The lawyer expected an answer that would make life manageable and the rule of law and Jewish custom performable. In the words of the scripture, he sought to "justify himself." But Jesus laid out a life larger than anybody could handle and an expectation for compliance with the law that could be fulfilled only by some action of God himself. What was to be heard in Jesus' parable—what Jesus evidently listened for and hoped those to whom he spoke might listen for—was a distinctive way to relate to God and to other people in the thick of life's most demanding, down-to-earth moments. To listen with Jesus to what he preached, therefore, was to be changed. [7]

Of course, not every one of Jesus' sermons was a parable. He spoke in proverbs at times. At other times he simply preached through conversation with people he met, as when he talked to the woman at the well in the Samaritan village of Sychar. On other occasions it would seem that he must have engaged in some form of more extended discourse. Perhaps his talk with his disciples in the upper room, shortly before his arrest and trial and crucifixion, could be considered one such preaching effort of greater length and complexity.

Likewise, preaching, ever since Jesus' time, has taken various forms and has been occasioned by various situations. There have been attempts to state suggestively, if not exhaustively, the many kinds of preaching that have developed. So we have heard of textual sermons, expository sermons, topical sermons, and doctrinal sermons, with formats ranging from informal chat to structured dialogue, to monological discourse, to storytelling, just to name a few! All sermons, however, regardless of type, have something in common; and what they have in common with each other, they also have in common with the sermons of Jesus. The common factor is the use of religious language.

To say that the language of preaching is religious, however, is not to say that it is technical, esoteric, and difficult. Theological language may be all those things. But theological language is not the same as religious language. Theological language is used to investigate the language of religious experience. It attempts to describe that language, sometimes called God talk, and to explain how it interacts with the experience it evokes. Theological language, therefore, must be as precise as possible. It is used self-consciously and critically; it is rule-conscious, not intuitive. To put it in a word, it is scientific. Religious language, on the other hand, is mundane—at times maybe even earthy—not to mention imprecise. And as I have noted, it functions to disclose new ways of thinking and being and doing to those who hear it. [8] It sometimes jars people out of their habitual patterns of thought, as Jesus' parable of the good Samaritan jarred the would-be self-righteous lawyer who originally heard it, and as that parable might jar us, had we the ears to hear it. To accomplish that jarring, however, no special terms had to be employed. No polysyllabic words of peculiar derivation had to be dredged up. And no multivolume dictionary had to be consulted by the listener in order for him to understand what was meant. Helmut Thielicke has suggested in *The Waiting Father*, in fact, that Jesus' very simplicity and directness and earthiness may have been what caused the lawyer who "stood up to put him to the test" his most acute embarrassment. It was the lawyer who wanted to be theological and correct. Jesus, however, wanted only to be profoundly responsive to what he saw as the lawyer's deep personal need. No, religious language is not esoteric, technical, scientific, and exclusive. Just the opposite, in fact, is the case: It is common, plain, evocative, and thoroughly inclusive. Preachers' biggest problem, therefore, never is to read themselves *into* a good sermon. Instead, the biggest problem is to figure how on earth to get *out* of it—how to escape the perhaps costly and uncomfortable change it would accomplish in them.

The religious language of the preacher is similar to the language of the poet, novelist, or dramatist. It is alive with the rhythms, accents, and images of ordinary speech. However, those elements of ordinary speech combine bits of experience for us in ways we might not expect, thereby provoking insight. Suddenly, because of what the poet says, the novelist says, the dramatist or preacher says, your world and mine, the world of everyday occurrences that we have named a thousand times, taken for granted, not given much thought to, lights up with significance. We see ourselves and we see our world more clearly than we may have seen it ever before, and we say, "That's right, that's it! That is my world as it is or could be or ought to be!"

To put it still another way, the religious language of preaching is metaphorical. Sallie TeSelle, a theologian at the divinity school of Vanderbilt University, has stated that all Jesus' parables, for example, are extended metaphors. [9] When they were heard (by those who had ears to hear), there always was a shock of recognition, people coming to awareness that their life was being depicted in those parables—their life as they actually lived it; their death, as they actually faced it, with anxiety, or anger, or pain, or grief. And yet the life depicted in Jesus' parables, and alluded to in his other discourses, also was life as another would have it: gracious, open, caring up to the hilt, and filled with wonders and terrors, not turned from but faced. Jesus' preaching rendered human life accessible to God. It disclosed to people the fact that, as C. H. Dodd put it, individuals' personal biographies, and human history itself, remain forever "plastic to the will of God."[10] They are susceptible to divine intervention.

The religious language of preaching today also is meant to be metaphorical. It does more than describe or explain reality; literal language can do that. The language of preaching, on the other hand, is aimed at *evoking* reality—or more precisely, some specific view of reality. Preaching is not just the proclamation of an event—even of The Event; it *is* an event—a happening, an experience. Sermons, of course, may contain statements that are literally true. Assertions may be made in preaching that are susceptible to verification or refutation; and, along with opinions, feelings, and convictions, facts may appear—references may be made to specific situations and people and objects. That is why, if any sermon is to be compelling, the preacher who speaks it must avoid misrepresentations of any kind. A sermon full of illogic and fabricated statistics, lacking verisimilitude, will not get and probably should not get a responsible hearing. But a sermon that does nothing more than indicate what already is, is really no sermon at all. Sermons that truly are sermons—preaching that in some way measures up to what preaching is meant to be—will take what is and will place it at the disposal of what God would have it be. Preaching issues a "claim," H. H. Farmer has said.[11] It directs us toward the future, and to Him to whom the future belongs. The referent of a sermon, therefore— what it refers or points to—is not something in the past, nor is it any individual, thing, or circumstance of the present. Instead, the referent of a sermon is what lies beyond. Preaching has to do with what yet may be.[12]

Preaching, of course, does not take place in a vacuum. It happens within the context of a specific community that possesses tradition, that is presently alive, and that continually is choosing new directions and purposes. Preaching seeks the transformation of the life of that community, and at the same time, it is continuous with that life. It envisions new possibilities for its people. Yet it does so with facts and images, the resources of the past and present of those people. The act of preaching employs memory and stimulates forethought. It involves analysis and prescription, and those who engage in it, preachers and listeners alike, therefore are required to exercise their capacity for empathy (reading themselves into actual or imaginary events of the past or present) and imagination (projecting future possibilities—extrapolation). Preachers who would listen carefully to what is happening in their sermons and who would have others do so with them, consequently must have one ear cocked in the direction of the Scriptures and the life represented therein, and the other in the direction of their peoples' developing history and present life and the various possibilities for grappling creatively with them. [13]

To aid preachers in this singularly demanding work of mind, will, and heart, there is one persistent, living metaphor that has provided critique and new life from biblical times to the present and that continues actively to engage the memory and the imagination of people both in pulpits and in pews today—the life and death and resurrection of the believing community's acknowledged Savior and Lord. Call it a *kerygma*. Call it what you will, but listen for it when you preach, for it will be there, explicitly or implicitly, doing its work, disclosing to you something of the significance of past events and opening up before you possibilities for the future.

Up to this point, I have attempted to indicate the utter necessity of preachers listening to their own sermons. I also have made an effort, through a description of the nature of the preaching event, to show why that listening is essential and how it ought to be done. Now I want to present four principles for the listening preacher, educed from the description of the nature and purpose of preaching just given.

First, attend to the movement of thought in preaching and be prepared to move with it, for preaching that is true preaching never will let you rest content with some static arrangement of ideas.

Second, attend to the specific contexts that give rise to the movement of thought in preaching and be aware of your personal involvement with them, for in preaching, ideas never are abstract. They are grounded in past, present, and emerging situations of human life.

Third, allow yourself to hear the claim made upon you when you preach. For preaching, after all, makes use of religious/metaphoric language, which has the power to disclose new ways—perhaps challenging, or even uncomfortable, but responsible ways—of being and acting in the world.

Last, listen for the explicit or implicit kerygma that gives coherence to the sermon as a whole and that sustains you in your effort to relate the world of religious experience evoked in scripture to the experience of people today.

Bear in mind that these principles are in fact *principles*, not *rules*. The manner of their implementation, therefore, is entirely up to you. The remaining chapters will lead you through guided explorations in the implementation of these four principles for the listening preacher, and it is hoped they will provide you with some guidance in speaking so as to facilitate the listening of others. But there is room for your own uniqueness, for after all, the preaching moment does not expect of you anything other, or more, or less, than what you have to give—yourself.

II. THE SOUND OF SENSE IN PREACHING

Delight
↗
Wisdom

> *Principle number one for the listening preacher: Attend to the movement of thought in preaching and be prepared to move with it, for preaching that is true preaching never will let you rest content with some static arrangement of ideas.*

The movement of thought in preaching is not always a movement of ideas. Sometimes it is attitudes that move, expressed as thoughts, of course—noted as occurrences by the mind. At other times, convictions, gut feelings we call them, march out to engage each other in timid or mortal combat.[1] Therefore, there is no easy attending to the movement of thought in preaching. Instead, such attending can be done only with effort. Robert Frost once said of his poems, for instance, that they began "in delight" and ended "in wisdom." Yet it would take work—mental effort—on a reader's part to enter Frost's delight, to discover Frost's wisdom, and to express both with clarity. The same could be said of any sermon, including your own. Where is the delight? Where the wisdom? And how does one get from one to the other with enough clarity of expression to enable others to follow? Your first task and your solemn joy in preaching is to accomplish those very things.

Here is a clue that may help you accomplish what you must:

Notice that in any movement of thought, there is conflict, or at least resistance; a point of resolution of that conflict; a climax; and a denouement. There may be a flight of fancy against some downdrag of literalism. There may be a will to find out a secret that some other will wants locked up forever. There may be a struggle to get a look at what is true, beautiful, and good, opposed by some love of what is false and ugly and wicked. And there always will be some point in your sermon or, for that matter, in someone's poem, essay, or story, where the flight is achieved, at least in part, or fails; where the secret is discovered or lost; or where the true, the beautiful, and the good are glimpsed or not seen at all.

Charlotte I. Lee, in discussing the oral interpretation of poetry, says that in the conflict of opposing forces, there is a point of turning, and she calls that point the "fulcrum" of a text.[2] The fulcrum is the place where the poem or, as I am using the concept, sermon, balances, if you will—half its weight resting on one side of the fulcrum, half on the other. The fulcrum may or may not be the exact center of the text, and it may or may not coincide with the climax. In any case, on one side of the fulcrum conflict develops in one particular way, while on the other side, the conflict develops differently. For fun, and for example, see if you can find the fulcrum in the following poem by A. R. Ammons.

Levitation

What are you doing
up there
said the ground
that disastrous to seers
and saints
is always around
evening scores, calling down:

I turned
cramped in abstraction's gilded loft
and
tried to think of something beautiful to say:

why
I said failing

I'm investigating the
coming together of things:

the ground
tolerant of such
widened without sound

while I turning
harmed my spine against
the peak's inner visionless ribs—

heels free
neck locked in the upward drift—

and even the ground I think
grew shaky
thinking something might be up there
able to get away. [3]

Let me be presumptuous—even cocky perhaps—and guess that on first reading you missed not only the conflict and the fulcrum, but nearly everything else that might have been there to find. The poem is not easy to read. There can be no mere skimming of it for its message, and there can be no giving of its message with a casual sounding of its words or a neat paraphrase of its contents; for its words and sounds, its content and form are tight, dense, almost opaque. You must engage the poem if you would hear it. You must let it work on you till it puts you where it wants you; till it makes of you what it will. You must finally become part of its world; and that is possible only through the closest reading you can manage and through paying attention to detail.

On one side of its fulcrum, the poem, although it does not indicate this with traditional punctuation, wants us to hear the voice of two opposing wills speaking to each other. The will of the poem's persona—its implied central character—speaks, telling us what has been going on between a personified "ground" and itself. [4] However, that persona also lets the ground speak: "What are you doing / up there," and replies, in turn, "I'm investigating the / coming together of things." The persona, in other words, wants to enter and stay up in a reverie of abstraction, while the ground (the persona's alter ego?) wants that persona down to earth, as it were. The conflict between the persona's intent and the ground's intent, however, loses one of its voices as "the ground / tolerant" of what the persona has just said, widens "without sound." From that point on, only the persona is heard, spelling out the conflict between itself and the ground, in words meant for our ears exclusively. We still are part of the conversation, but the ground is out of it. The fulcrum, the place of turning in the development of conflict in the poem, then, can be found where the phrase "the ground / tolerant of such / widened without sound" occurs. Interestingly, in this particular poem, the fulcrum does appear at very nearly the precise middle of the text.

Try reading the poem again, slowly, carefully, out loud, identifying yourself as closely as you can with the poem's persona. Hear yourself speaking to your listeners—or let them overhear you speaking to yourself—and hear yourself speaking to the ground, as well, of your investigation of "the coming together of things"; hear yourself indicating, as with the ground's own voice, how it toys with you, tolerating your reverie, but still patiently waiting and willing to have you down from your lofty contemplation. Then after the fulcrum—the turning point—in your conflict with the ground has been reached, speak as though you meant what you were saying to be heard only by your listeners, the ground surely part of your awareness, but just as surely left out of your conversation. Feel your back arch up "against the peak's inner visionless ribs," your heels hang down into the air—as if they could—and your neck lock in an "upward drift." In other words, give your body to your thoughts. You see! You are in the poem's world yourself, and very nearly have become its persona! And the experience of the persona is in you. Can't you tell? Why, you have almost made the ground doubt its own inevitable claim upon you and your thoughts. You have almost made it think, perhaps, if only for a moment, that your reverie in abstraction can be sustained, that the "seer," the "saint" in you, will not be called down to disaster, that "something might be up there able to get away."

Now I suspect, and I am sure you are utterly convinced, that no sermon of yours, however finely crafted, ever will have the tight, thick opaqueness of this poem. The turning point in the development of conflict—the fulcrum of your text—no doubt will be more self-evident; and the climax of your clashing thoughts and the denouement that follows will be simpler and more predictable, even if less dramatic and compelling. And not least of all, you probably never will have so peculiar an end in mind for those who attend to your sermons, or for yourself, as the remembrance of your momentary defeat of earth's powers to ground human reflection on "the coming together of things." To put it bluntly, your sermons will not be poems, at least not very often, and there is no reason at all to expect any preacher to be a poet. Still, your sermons will have conflict, if they are to have life at all, and that conflict will need to be heard and felt by those who listen. The fulcrum of your text will need to be discerned, the climax lived through, and the denouement, if possible, enjoyed. And believe it, at least on some occasions, your sermons may be more opaque than you imagined they could be. The movement of thought in your preaching may be easier to follow than the movement of thought in a poem, but the expression of that movement, so that others may hear and follow it, still will take some close "reading" on your part, and no little attention to detail.

Following are three exercises specifically pertaining to the movement of thought in preaching. Work through them all, for each presents a unique challenge to the reader/preacher in the development of conflict; in the location of the fulcrum, or turning point, in that development; and in the handling of climax and denouement.

The first exercise is a terse homiletical definition of anger by the contemporary novelist/essayist/homiletician, Frederick Buechner. The conflict, an implied one, fought out in the "innards" of every human being, is the conflict between one's almost greedy affection for anger, and one's dismay, even repulsion, at its devastating power. The fulcrum is found in the third sentence of the text; and there the climax is to be found as well. The denouement, one sentence long, is artistically satisfying, and for that reason it is in a sense enjoyable; yet at the same time it is emotionally discomfiting. *Anger*, in its quiet, reflective way, is meant to appall. In your reading of it, see that it does. Pause a little longer just before the words "The chief drawback," for that is the fulcrum and the climax. Then pause again before the last sentence, the denouement. See if that doesn't help you to feel the appalling nature of the conflict developed by Buechner in this text.

Of the Seven Deadly Sins, anger is possibly the most fun. To lick your wounds, to smack your lips over grievances long past, to roll over your tongue the prospect of bitter confrontations still to come, to savor to the last toothsome morsel both the pain you are given and the pain you are giving back—in many ways it is a feast fit for a king. The chief drawback is that what you are wolfing down is yourself. The skeleton at the feast is you.[5]

The reading of *The Patriot*, by Robert Browning, is your second exercise. Of course, Browning's poem is not a sermon; it is a poem, and a great one, and one that a great many people know and love. Yet it may be considered preaching of a kind, for its purpose is discernibly homiletical, its intent suasive. It offers a theological interpretation of life through its persona's experience and presents a complex character of faith as compelling as any hero of the Bible. In *The Patriot*, victory is snatched out of the jaws of defeat, certainly hope out of despair, and perhaps even life out of death. The conflict in the poem is of a threefold nature. There is the conflict between what the persona, the patriot whom we hear speaking (or more accurately, whom we overhear thinking), deserves, and what he gets from the crowd of his admirers turned accusers. There is the conflict within the persona between the outrage or bitterness or fear and self-pity that his circumstances would seem to require, and the calm that his apparent faith, or at least his religious insight, at last enables him to achieve. And there is the conflict of time, past with present— the way it was, playing with devastating clarity against the way it is. The fulcrum is not hard to locate. It can be found in the precise middle of the text, where these words occur: "There's nobody on the housetops now." The preceding three stanzas were all past tense; the remaining three are present. The climax and the denouement both appear in the final stanza, in which the patriot, in full realization of the cruelly ironic contrast between his former status in the minds of his friends—"Thus I entered"—and his present status—"and thus I go"—is satisfied with a security that those who have "dropped down dead" at the height of their triumph and adulation may not have been so fortunate to enjoy. His security is in knowing or intuiting that the reward he is to receive will be presented to him from the hand and heart of God, and not from any mere human crowd,

admiring or otherwise. And as is said in the poem itself, he is "safer
so." As with the Ammons poem, your job is to identify with the
persona—in this case, the patriot. Feel what he feels; think what he
thinks; do what he does. Don't hurry! After all, you are on your way
to the scaffold. (This final bit of help: The word "trow" simply means
"suppose," or "believe.")

The Patriot

It was roses, roses, all the way,
    With myrtle mixed in my path like mad:
The house-roofs seemed to heave and sway,
    The church-spires flamed, such flags they had,
A year ago on this very day.

The air broke into a mist with bells,
    The old walls rocked with the crowd and cries.
Had I said, "Good folk, mere noise repels—
    But give me your sun from yonder skies!"
They had answered, "And afterward, what else?"

Alack, it was I who leaped at the sun
    To give it my loving friends to keep!
Naught man could do, have I left undone:
    And you see my harvest, what I reap
This very day, now a year is run.

There's nobody on the house-tops now—
    Just a palsied few at the windows set;
For the best of the sight is, all allow,
    At the Shambles' Gate—or, better yet,
By the very scaffold's foot, I trow.

I go in the rain, and, more than needs,
    A rope cuts both my wrists behind;
And I think, by the feel, my forehead bleeds,
    For they fling, whoever has a mind,
Stones at me for my year's misdeeds.

Thus I entered, and thus I go!
    In triumphs, people have dropped down dead.
"Paid by the world, what dost thou owe
    Me?"—God might question; now instead,
'Tis God shall repay: I am safer so.

Your last exercise in the movement of thought in preaching is the following sermon. Study it and practice it aloud. I wrote the sermon, and I have used it here not because of its intrinsic worth, but because it illustrates clearly and simply the principles explored in this chapter. When you have satisfied yourself that you know how you want to express its movement of thought, record it on tape, as if you were delivering it to some group of listeners. When you play it back, see if you can hear yourself moving up to the fulcrum, or point of crisis, where the development of conflict in the sermon tips into a new dimension or where it takes on a different kind of expression. Listen also to discover whether your experience of the climax and resolution of the conflict can be felt. In reading, consider yourself an interested narrator, moved by the subject of your narration, but not necessarily identified with him. I have labeled the fulcrum, climax, and resolution, or denouement, in order to facilitate your preparation. The sermon is in story form, but it *is* a sermon. The text upon which it is based is Mark 10:17-22—Jesus' encounter with the rich young ruler. It is not based upon an exegesis of the *content* of that encounter, however. Rather it reflects the *nature,* or *form*, of the encounter. *How* the rich young ruler responded to Jesus is the basis for the narrative character study you must preach. I would suggest that you read through the sermon once, simply to become familiar with it. Then read it aloud, noting particularly the fulcrum, climax, and denouement. Finally, practice your delivery three, four, or more times until you frankly feel overly familiar with it. Then you will be ready to record.

Safe from Acts of God

Whatever it was that Robert Ransom Merrill lacked, none of us could imagine. He lived where we all dreamed of living, high atop the nearest of the Watchung Hills. His house was brand new, but looked old yet well kept across the years, so cleverly had the builders worked to produce an authentic colonial appearance.

Down the steep of his crushed-stone drive, falling away on each side, green manicured lawns stretched, hardwood-fastened to sloping dirt and rock. Not a speck of soil, not a needle of grass could ever be dislodged from its place on that hill, even if it had the will.

What Robert Ransom Merrill owned, he kept safe from wind, rain, melting snow, or *any* acts of God.

He kept himself safe, too. He would not blunder into any tempting of the fates. Gracious, clean living, that's what he was after always; he said so himself.

He ran his business to the letter of the law; took care of his wife and family. In every way he was a most agreeable man.

He was young enough to be attractive without needing to be handsome, and he was kind enough to be respected without having to wear his caring on his sleeve.

He was circumspect, but not a prude; amiable, but never garrulous. He made promises seldom, but what promises he made, he kept.

Robert Ransom Merrill was a man of his word—there was no doubting it. Never once did he bluster. What he said he would do, he did.

He said he would tithe, for instance, so he tithed; every year (For God's sake? His own? No matter.) he tithed, giving away a tenth of all he had earned; giving significant gifts to his church, to community projects, and to charities in which he believed.

He always paid his taxes, too—local, state and federal—never once turning in less than was required, to the last cent. He did not believe in what we call cutting corners or working angles. Honor, for him, was not a matter of words and show, but of deeds. His conscience was as clear as anybody's conscience could be. And his reputation was spotless. With him, no one ever found fault.

It was all the more surprising, therefore, that he should have found fault with himself. Nevertheless, there he was, one summer's night, Robert Ransom Merrill, tossing and turning in bed, ill at ease in his comforts, vexed about his life.

Fulcrum

"Oh, you wouldn't understand if I tried to tell you," he thought. "Nobody would understand."

His wife did not reply. She was asleep; and anyway, Robert

Ransom Merrill was not actually talking to her, or even out loud. He was talking to . . well . . . himself, as he often did when perplexed. As *we* do. He was trying to grasp he knew not what, and to keep it, he knew not how.

His talking went on. "What's the use of it—life? Where's the meaning in doing, caring, paying, keeping, giving? In all the world, is there anything big enough to love and keep for good? We cannot even care for and keep *ourselves* for good, can we?

"You can feel it slip away—life. You can feel it tug at your heart—tug away from it, as if to lose itself to somewhere or something or someone.

"So your heart beats—for what? Can anybody say? And your eyes tear—for what? And your smile breaks out from cheek to cheek—for what?"

Climax

"Dare I—dare I think of giving it up for good, all of it, not just some of it, not 10, but 100 percent? Should I rip it free from my heart and fling it away, and so be rid of the tug?

"And if I do that, to whom do I fling it, or to what? To God? To some black hole in the center of the universe that someday will suck everything into oblivion? To grim death, to the noiseless, patient yawn of the grave? *That's* as likely—*more* likely, maybe!

"All that I have, do, care about, kept forever by some other—by something or nothing—to do with what nobody can tell? I couldn't have that! Shouldn't have that! House, family, work, getting, giving, paying, keeping, crying, laughing—how can I give them up? They are *mine*! They are all I have! They are what I am!"

Denouement

Robert Ransom Merrill's discomfiture with himself did not go on and on, of course. After the talking and tossing and turning, there was at last a troubled sleep. And then a new day, with new moments of tears and smiles, caring for the lawn, giving to the church, and the rest.

His house still sits upon that Watchung Hill—and, oh yes, the house is *his*; and his business still runs according to Hoyle and his decency is intact. Everybody likes him, just as I said before. Robert Ransom Merrill is as agreeable as anyone could be. That's the way it has always been. That's the way it ever *shall* be.

Life *should* be kept safe from acts of God, from the crashing thunders of rain, from dripping rains of grief, and from the melting snows of hate.

Robert Ransom Merrill lives graciously and cleanly, taking care to keep well what is his, and giving where he can, to help others keep what is theirs.

What more could a person want, than what Mr. Merrill has?

III. PREACHING AND THE IMAGINATIONS OF THE HEART

Principle number two for the listening preacher: Attend to the specific context that gives rise to the movement of thought in preaching and be aware of your personal involvement with them, for in preaching, ideas never are abstract. They are grounded in past, present, and emerging situations of human life.

If, as indicated in the previous chapter, preachers are to listen to the movement of thought in their sermons and be prepared to move with it, then it seems no less incumbent upon them, I should think, to listen to whatever gives rise to that movement of thought. People do not just talk, after all; they are coaxed or jarred into it. People do not just preach, either. Something motivates them—something woos and wins, or provokes their homiletical efforts. Of course, ultimately, basically, and most profoundly, that something is an encounter with God; but more specifically, immediately, and concretely, it is the clustering of facts, opinions, attitudes, convictions, events, and ideas that mediate the encounter. Every sermon is full of such things, as the world itself is full of them. Donald E. Phillips, for instance, commenting upon Karl Barth's thought relative to existential communication and dialectic, said,

Reality in both its objective (phenomenal) and subjective (existential) aspects inherently communicates and summons communication. The phenomenal universe presents myriads of objects which confront us, claim our attention, energy, time, and demand interpretation, assimilation, ordering, and decision.[1]

There is nothing in preaching to which we can be unresponsive. We may be indifferent toward something—some idea we have just put into words or some anecdote we have used to illustrate that idea—but indifference, of course, is a response. So is neutrality; so is boredom; so is unfettered, wild excitement. Particularly when it comes to preaching, the truth of what people say "depends on the depth of their engagement rather than the height of their detachment."[2] The word "truth" there, of course, means authenticity or sincerity, not simply literal accuracy. What preachers surely want as much as, if not more than, anything else, is to be true both to themselves and to that about which they feel called upon to speak. They want to be honest, not dishonest. They want to be credible, not incredible. In other words, they have no intention of putting on an act.[3]

Yet *wanting* to be authentic, sincere, and credible is not enough. One also must know *how* to be these things. And let us be clear about this—authenticity is not simply a function of self-disclosure. You will say a good deal about yourself—even about that deepest self with whom you may be personally quite unfamiliar—whenever you preach, and you will do so inadvertently; for, as Walter J. Ong has pointed out, the spoken word has a unique capacity to reveal what he calls your "interiority."[4] You need not make an effort to show it. Who you are, sooner or later, for better or for worse, *will* appear of its own accord. How you feel at the moment of preaching—whether you have a toothache; whether you have an especially sour mood running through you, like blood through your veins; whether you have just had a verbal circus with members of your family or with your friends; or whether you've had a particularly grueling time preparing your sermon—all that, you need not confess, either directly or indirectly, when you are in the pulpit. You are not there to display the sorry or happy state of your health—physical, emotional, or spiritual. You are not there even to indicate the unassailable character of your faith or the perversity or blessedness of your doubts. You are there to *preach*, and that means putting yourself at the disposal of everything in your sermon that possibly can call for response from you: the ideas, the words, figures, anecdotes, and stories that make it up. Responding *appropriately* to what your sermon may expect of you and of your listeners—that is what will be required of you, if your desire, above all else, is to be sincere.

If, in a handball game, both your palms puffed and aching, your shoulders knotted in pain, your knees trembling and threatening to "cave in" and let you down hard on the court, you take one mighty last swing at that nasty little ball and miss, and lose the match, you do not politely, gently, and circumspectly say, "Oh dear, I've lost it," do you? I suspect something just a bit more earthy and emphatic would be your likely response. Or if, in conversation, you remember the details of a splendid party you attended, you do not list them all with dutiful accuracy, objectivity, and neutrality, do you? Rather, your face lights up from chin to hairline—despite the splitting headache or pesky postnasal drip that may be tormenting you at the moment—and with joy in your throat and lightness in your heart, you let what happened at that party very nearly happen once more, don't you? Why not, then, let something similar happen when you preach? Why not let your sermon live?

Once Harry Emerson Fosdick, tired of war, weary of the memory of serving as a chaplain to the troops, said in a sermon,

> In the Bible we read terrible passages where the Hebrews thought they had command from Jehovah to slaughter the Amalekites, "both man and woman, infant and suckling, ox and sheep, camel and ass." Dreadful! we say, an ancient and appalling idea! Ancient? Appalling? Upon the contrary, that is war, and always will be. A military order, issued in our generation by an American general in the Philippines and publicly acknowledged by his counsel afterwards in military court, commanded his soldiers to burn and kill, to exterminate all capable of bearing arms, and to make the island of Samar a howling wilderness. Moreover, his counsel acknowledged that he had specifically named the age of ten with instructions to kill every one over that. Far from launching into a denunciation of that American general, I am much more tempted to state his case for him. Why not? Cannot boys and girls of eleven fire a gun?

Why not kill everything over ten? That is war, past, present and future. All that our modern fashions have done is to make the necessity of slaughtering children not the comparatively simple and harmless matter of shooting some of them in Samar, one by one, but the wholesale destruction of children, starving them by millions, impoverishing them, spoiling the chances of unborn generations of them, as in the Great War. [5]

That's what Dr. Fosdick had to say to himself and to those who had come to hear him. Can you imagine anyone saying such words as if they didn't matter; as if the words had nothing better to do than to leave people—preachers and listeners alike—exactly as they found them? Not likely! If we would learn to preach the truth—if we would speak with authenticity—then we must learn to let what we have to say speak to us until it has produced some change in us—until it has called forth from us some response. We must learn to talk with color. We must learn to think imagistically!

Speaking our words with color enables people to hear not only the words' denotation—what they mean as defined in the dictionary— but also their connotation—what they mean to us in the context in which they appear. Some words very nearly color themselves, of course. They are called onomatopoetic words. They sound so much like the things they represent that with very minimal effort, a speaker can pronounce them interestingly and provocatively. Here is a list of such onomatopoetic words. [6] Say them aloud and listen for the action they represent.

Onomatopoetic Words

buzz	**babble**	**pinch**
hiss	**scratch**	**roll**
bang	**slither**	**strut**

Did you notice that you lengthened the sounds of some of the words a bit as you said them with color? Did you notice that in pronouncing some—"babble" and "scratch," for instance—it was the vowel sounds that were stretched most, whereas in others, such as "hiss" and "buzz," the continuent consonant sounds were stretched? And did you notice that other words almost forced abruptness on you—"bang," "pinch," "strut"? Words do expect something of you, don't they? And they expect more than just vocal response—they expect physical action as well! You cannot say "pinch" with your lips simply hanging over your teeth. And you cannot say "strut" with your shoulders hunched forward and your chest caved in, unless, of course, you mean to parody the word. (There are circumstances where you may wish to speak a word with vocal and physical gesture seemingly contradictory to the word's rather obvious meaning. That, however, will depend upon compositional context, a matter we will consider later.)

Here are words that sound similar, but have colors that clash. Speak them aloud, remembering to respond to the words both vocally and physically. With your voice and your body, be and do what the words imply.

Words That Clash

quick—sick	consolation—desolation
sly—shy	inspire—tire
gay—gray	cheer—fear
hope—mope	vicious—precious
clean—obscene	excited—blighted

Were you able to hear the differences in action and condition? Were you able to feel those differences? Did they take shape in your body? If not, you might try saying the words once more, this time exaggerating your response.

As a final exercise in word color, say the following phrases with appropriate vocal response and physical gesture. The words in the parentheses are not to be spoken. Those comments, as must be self-evident, are meant to indicate exactly how the exercises should *not* be read.

Word Color

A. I remember it was in the bleak December . . .
    (*Not* the Fourth of July.)

B. Goliath of Gath, whose height was six cubits and a span . . .
    (*Not* five feet and nine inches.)

C. An aged thrush, frail, gaunt, and small . . .
    (*Not* a sixty-pound vulture with a nine-foot wing span.)

D. She walks in beauty, like the night
    Of cloudless climes and starry skies . . .
    (She does *not* drive a diesel truck through the Holland
       Tunnel.)

E. Belshazzar the King made a great feast to a thousand of his
       lords,
    and drank wine before the thousand.
    (*Not* a dietetic brunch with his secretary.)[7]

Saying your words with color will be easier, I suspect, if you will learn to think imagistically. Re-create for yourself, as you speak, the sensations indicated by the linguistic symbols appearing on a page or lodged in your brain. There are sight images, sound images, olfactory images, gustatory images, tactile, visceral, and kinesthetic images.[8] If your thoughts are to come alive as you express them, therefore, you must see or hear them, smell or taste them, feel or let them churn inside you. Or you may need to go along with the movement of them, tensing or relaxing your muscles as you speak. No doubt you will not always literally have gone through every kind of sensation that might be indicated by what you say in a sermon. Still, you have smelled enough, seen enough, heard, felt, and done enough to be moved to an inner experience that is at least very similar to those things about which you may be speaking. To be able to read ourselves into events, situations, or states of being that are fictional, or that have not actually happened to us personally, is a capacity very nearly all of us have been gifted with, else we could not "rejoice with those who rejoice [and] weep with those who weep" (Rom. 12:15). We are capable of empathic response. Utilizing your capacity for empathy, then, read yourself into the experiences suggested by the following brief passages. As you say the words, do more than simply look at them. Concentrate on seeing, or hearing, or feeling what the passages intend you to see, or hear, or feel.

Sight Images

(A harassed village "bum" is returned from would-be sobriety to drunkenness.)

You would see the press go out of his suit as the slouch came back into his shoulders. You could watch the stubble and grime come back on his chin as the proud little blue lights went out in his eyes. He would seem to wilt visibly under the brutal barrage from the curbstone wits.[9]

Sound Images

Reedy monotones of locust, or sounds of katydid—I hear the latter at night, and the other both day and night. I thought the morning and evening warble of birds delightful; but I find I can listen to these strange insects with just as much pleasure. A single locust is now heard near noon from a tree two hundred feet off, as I write—a long whirring, continued, quite loud noise graded in distinct whirls, or swinging circles, increasing in strength and rapidity up to a certain point, and then a fluttering, quiet tapering fall. Each strain is continued from one to two minutes. The locust-song is very appropriate to the scene—gushes, has meaning, is masculine, is like some fine old wine, not sweet, but far better than sweet.[10]

Olfactory Images

Here's the smell of the blood still; all the perfumes of Arabia will not sweeten this little hand.[11]

. . .

Even Saint Nicholas, in his turn,
Gives off a faint and reminiscent stench,
The merest soupçon, of brimstone and the pit.[12]

. . .

Then [Jacob's] father Isaac said to him, "Come near and kiss me, my son." So he came near and kissed him; and he smelled the smell of his garments, and blessed him, and said,
    "See, the smell of my son
    is as the smell of a field which the Lord has blessed."[13]

Gustatory Images

The towheads were crazy about hamburgers. And so was [Jeff York's] wife, for that matter. You could tell it, even if she didn't say anything, for she would lift her bowed-forward head a little, and her face would brighten, and she would run her tongue out to wet her lips just as the plate with the hamburger would be set . . . before her. But all those folks, like Jeff York and his family, like hamburgers, with pickle and onions and mustard and tomato catsup, the whole works. . . . They have to swallow to keep the mouth from flooding before they even take the first bite.[14]

Tactile Images

Forth from the well [the rats] hurried in fresh troops . . . and leaped in hundreds upon my person. The measured movement of the pendulum disturbed them not at all. Avoiding its strokes, . . . they pressed—they swarmed upon me in ever accumulating heaps. They writhed upon my throat; their cold lips sought my own. I was half stifled by their thronging pressure; . . . with a more than human resolution I lay still.[15]

Visceral Images

He who dwells in the shelter of
    the Most High,
who abides in the shadow of the
    Almighty,
Will say to the Lord, "My refuge and
    my fortress;
    My God, in whom I trust."
For he will deliver you from the snare of the fowler
    and from the deadly pestilence;
he will cover you with his pinions,
    and under his wings you will find refuge;
    his faithfulness is a shield and buckler.
You will not fear the terror of the night,
    nor the arrow that flies by day,
nor the pestilence that stalks in darkness,
    nor the destruction that wastes at noonday.[16]

Kinesthetic Images

> He always kept his poise
> To the top branches, climbing carefully
> With the same pains you use to fill a cup
> Up to the brim, and even above the brim.
> Then he flung outward, feet first, with a swish,
> Kicking his way down through the air to the ground.
> So was I once myself a swinger of birches.
> And so I dream of going back to be.[17]

· · ·

Now that you've become acquainted with the processes of imagistic thought and with speaking your words with color, the time has come to attempt to do your imaginative thinking and colorful speaking in a specific compositional context, for what a word or phrase suggests to you is determined not only by your previous experience of its use, but by its use in the present context. For example, in *The Patriot*, which we discussed earlier, the opening words seem to suggest a very "up-beat" experience. Therefore, it would appear that the words ought to be said with some excitement and exhilaration: "It was roses, roses, all the way!" However, the fact is that the person saying those words (or thinking them) is on his way to the scaffold. The roses are a memory only, and a bitter memory, at that. As Browning himself put it, "There's nobody on the housetops now." Consequently, the roses should be spoken about not with exhilaration, but with steel-jawed, ironic intent. Each poem, each story, anecdote, essay, or sermon provides a specific compositional context for the words used in it. So if we are to speak words with appropriate color, we must remain sensitive to compositional context, and responsive to it, as we are responsive to every word or phrase that we may speak.

Here is a poem that tells of the "cost and pain" of "making a poet out of a man." The persona of the poem, a third-person narrator, omniscient but not disinterested, observes the mythic god, Pan, ripping a reed from a river bed and cutting, gutting, and notching the

reed until a musical instrument is formed, through which "piercing
sweet," "blinding sweet" notes can be blown. The persona, with
whom we as readers are to identify, speaks with the intention of
having us share in a kind of perplexed fascination with what the god,
Pan, is up to, then a wonder-filled appreciation of the results of his
labors, and finally an experience of near grief over what has
happened to the reed (that is, the man-become-poet). The basic
attitude with which you are to speak of what you see and hear, then,
is fascination, moving toward awe, then trailing off into pathetic
reflection. Let each detail of sight and sound and action and reaction
you perceive in this poem, therefore, contribute to that movement.
Remembering what was discussed in chapter 2, take note of the
poem's fulcrum, climax, and denouement. The fulcrum occurs
with the opening words of the fifth stanza. There the persona's
fascination begins to turn to awe. The climax is achieved in stanza 6.
The seventh and last stanza, where the persona's awe changes to
pathetic reflection, is the denouement. As you speak of what you see
and hear in this event of making of a poet out of a man, be sure that
your sight and hearing is keen; use the inner eye and ear of your
imagination. And through empathic response, try to feel what the
persona felt. With the "true gods," sigh, if you will, "for the cost and
pain,/ For the reed which grows never more again/ As a reed with the
reeds in the river."

A *Musical Instrument*
(in original 1897 layout)

I.

What was he doing, the great god Pan,
    Down in the reeds by the river?
Spreading ruin and scattering ban,
Splashing and paddling with hoofs of a
        goat,
And **breaking the golden lilies afloat**
    With the dragon-fly on the river.

II.

He tore out a reed, the great god Pan,
　From the deep cool bed of the river:
The limped water turbidly ran,
And the broken lilies a-dying lay,
And the dragon-fly had fled away,
　Ere he brought it out of the river.

III.

High on the shore sat the great god Pan
　While turbidly flowed the river;
And hacked and hewed as a great god can,
With his hard bleak steel at the patient
　　reed,
Till there was not a sign of a leaf indeed
　To prove it fresh from the river.

IV.

He cut it short, did the great god Pan,
　(How tall it stood in the river!)
Then drew the pith, like the heart of a man,
Steadily from the outside ring,
And notched the poor dry empty thing
　In holes, as he sat by the river.

V.

"This is the way," laughed the great god Pan
(Laughed while he sat by the river),
"The only way, since gods began
To make sweet music, they could succeed."
Then, dropping his mouth to a hole in the
　　reed,
He blew in power by the river.

VI.

Sweet, sweet, sweet, O Pan!
　Piercing sweet by the river!
Blinding sweet, O great god Pan!
The sun on the hill forgot to die,

And the lilies revived, and the dragon-fly
Came back to dream on the river.

VII.

Yet half a beast is the great god Pan,
    To laugh as he sits by the river,
Making a poet out of a man:
The true gods sigh for the cost and pain,
For the reed which grows nevermore again
    As a reed with the reeds in the river.[18]

.   .   .

Your last task in this chapter on word color, imagistic thought, and empathy in preaching, is to read the following edited excerpt from a sermon on forgiveness by Harry Emerson Fosdick and let it live, as you did Elizabeth Barrett Browning's poem. Obviously, you are to identify with the preacher, who is trying to make clear just how tough forgiveness can be. The intent must determine your response to every word you speak. There is illustrative material, there are descriptions, anecdotal and biblical references, but the illustrative material is not to be indulged in for its own sake. Its significance is relative to the role it plays in making this point: Forgiveness never comes easy. Picturing must take place; words must be spoken with color; but above all, it is the point of the sermon that must affect you, move you, convince you. Listen for it with every syllable. When you have practiced aloud several times, record yourself speaking this homiletical excerpt. Then play back the recording and ask yourself these questions: Can the movement of thought be discerned? Is there an aliveness to the way thoughts are expressed? Is the point of the sermon made and felt?

Forgiveness of Sins

To condone sin is easy; to forgive it is hard. . . .

Here lies a familiar difference between two kinds of mothers. Some mothers have no moral depth, no moral seriousness. A superficial affectionateness distinguishes their motherhood. They have an instinctive maternity for their offspring, such as bears have for their cubs or birds for their fledglings. When the son of such a mother becomes a prodigal and wallows in vice, she will receive him again—will receive him, condoning his sin, making light of it, saying that it does not matter, making up more excuses for it than he ever could himself concoct. But some of us had mothers who never would have forgiven us that way. They would have forgiven us, but, alike for them and for us, it would have been serious. They would have borne upon their hearts the outrage of our sin as though they had committed it themselves. They would have gone with vicarious steps to the gateway of any hell we turned our feet toward and stood grief-stricken at the door till we came out. They would have put themselves in our places, lived in our stead, felt upon their innocence the burden of our guilt. They would have forgiven us but it would have turned their hair gray. That is forgiveness. It always means self-substitution. . . . And it is not easy. . . .

So in the Gospels you find it hard for Jesus. He was tremendously severe upon the scribes and Pharisees, you say, and truly he was. But what is the reason? Does it not reveal itself in verses like this, "Beware of the scribes . . . they that devour widows' houses, and for a pretence make long prayers"? Jesus was thinking of the widows and what the rapacity of the rulers did to them. His mother was a widow. We never hear of Joseph after Jesus' early boyhood. He knew what it was for a woman to be left with a family of children. More than once in Jesus' ministry a widow appeared, like the widow of Nain, and always his special gentleness overflowed. When in a parable he wanted to represent need, he pictured a widow pleading with an unjust judge. When, therefore, he was hard on scribes, one surmises the figure of his mother in the background of his mind. "They that devour widows' houses"—that made it hard to forgive. . . .

My friends, forgiveness is [a] miracle. The first thing that we are sure of in this universe is law. Some one has said that we can no more have sin without punishment than we can have positive electricity at one end of a needle without negative electricity at the other. And it would take more than a light-hearted chatterer condoning sin to convince me that there is anything else here. Too cheap! Too easy! But when I face Christ I face one whose plummet reached to the bottom of sin. Nobody ever took it so seriously; nobody ever hated it so for what it did to people, and yet he taught forgiveness. That is the miracle: that he taught forgiveness, that he practiced it so marvelously that no poor human wreck was beyond the reach of its benedictions; and that throughout Christian history the glory of the gospel has been men and women reclaimed by pardon to a reëstablished fellowship with God. It is marvelous good news. There is a merciful side to God and he forgives, but it is a miracle. Never take it lightly. "Which is easier, to say, Thy sins are forgiven thee; or to say, Arise and walk?"[19]

IV. HEARING WHAT PREACHING EXPECTS OF US

Principle number three for the listening preacher: Allow yourself to hear the "claim" made upon you when you preach. For preaching, after all, makes use of religious metaphoric language, which has the power to disclose new ways—perhaps challenging, or even uncomfortable, but responsible ways—of being and acting in the world.

Earlier, you read a sermon based on Jesus' encounter with the rich young ruler. The young man's problem, as you know, was not that he was rich, but that he was wholly unwilling, ever, under any circumstance, to become poor. Even though his refusal to sell all, to give up effective control of everything he had, would deny him a stable purpose and an end to his anxiety about life; even though his refusal to resign lordship over his own affairs would keep him distant from God, he still would refuse, for he had become identified with what he possessed to the point that he could not tolerate any thought of being dispossessed. He had very nearly become what he owned. Loss of possessions and loss of control meant loss of self. In a real sense, therefore, the rich young ruler did not possess anything. Instead, he was possessed *by* things. He was in a rut and could not get out of it; his future had been sealed off, and he could not enter it. Despite his wealth, he was "wretched, pitiable, poor, blind and naked" (Rev. 3:17). In Christina Rossetti's phrase, he could only say to himself, "What I was I am, I am even I."[1] Tragic! Whatever might have become of him had already happened, he thought. Consequently, "tomorrow, and tomorrow, and tomorrow [had to creep] in its petty pace."[2] Worse yet, now that he had been confronted by Jesus, he was aware of his plight as he never had been before—*fully* aware—not just in possession of "head" knowledge, but in possession of "gut" knowledge as well. The game was over! Life was done! Death owned him, and he knew it. So he went away "sorrowful."

Of course, there are *poor* young rulers too, and some among the so-called middle classes. In fact, young rulers (and old ones) abound in every circumstance of life. As Helmut Thielicke has put it, most of us, most of the time, concern ourselves with building little kingdoms and ruling them; "walling in or walling out"[3]; sealing ourselves off from any serious threat of hate or promise of love; trying desperately, often and anywhere, if not always and everywhere, to be the "gods of God."[4] Dead futures seem to be *our* lot no less than the lot of certain biblical characters. I heard that a famous author while seriously ill was asked, "Is there anything you want?" And he replied, "I want God." Don't we all?! Yet we refuse him, too, and will not accept him, for we cannot accept him and still be gods unto ourselves. So a mortal dilemma confronts us preachers and those who listen to us. Frederick Buechner has called that dilemma our homiletical "tragedy."[5]

The story is told of a homiletics professor who, many years ago, asked his classes, "What is the purpose of preaching?" His students would struggle valiantly to make adequate reply, but they never succeeded. Then, triumphantly, the professor would sing out, Scottish brogue and all, so I am told, "Gentlemen" (in his day there were only gentlemen would-be preachers), "the purpose of preaching is to raise the dead!" Perhaps the statement strikes us today as a bit florid and dramatic. Yet the professor was on to something that needs to be repeated again and again, I believe: When we preach, God registers his claim upon us. He breaks into the little kingdoms we have built, in which we attempt to exercise our rule over people and things, and says, "Let God be God."[6] He disturbs us in our comforts and presumptions, and—for what cause save his own graciousness, none of us can guess—quickens our dead future.

He does so with his Word—his *dābar*, his *logos*. As Peter Hodgson has pointed out, both the Hebrew *dābar* and the Greek *logos* imply dynamic, creative power: the power to bring into one's purview what was not there before; the power to select and arrange, to order and locate people and things—the cosmos itself![7] God has power to create worlds, including worlds of meaning, and in exercising that power, he discloses his own nature, revealing his anticipation of a world that could be called "good" (Gen. 1:1-31). He even designates a means of accessibility to himself. In order to bring us to himself he gives us worlds to contend with, and now and then in our travels through them, we may say, as Jacob said when he awoke from his troubled yet wonderful and awesome dream, "Surely the Lord is in this place; and I did not know it" (Gen. 28:16).

Even when we have not struggled very valiantly to live up to what preaching expects of us, God speaks his Word perhaps even in our own preaching, introduces us to his priorities, and makes clear to us what he would have us be about. He exercises his lordship over our lives. He breaks in upon our dreams with the actuality of his presence. He makes himself accessible to us. He lets us know that we are never our own, least of all when we think we are, or pretend that we are. And he lets us know that we are never *on* our own. Buechner calls that surprising accessibility of God our homiletical "comedy."[8] Despite the rich or poor, young or old rulers in us, who would have everything their own way, there is a God who insinuates himself into our affairs just so that he can direct traffic *his* way. He establishes contact with us, though that point of contact usually is a point of conflict. God takes us as we are, kicking or screaming or just obstinate or unaware, as the case may be, and as a great preacher, Paul Scherer, has noted, he conscripts us into the service as what he would have us be.[9] He makes our world—our worlds—his own. He makes them fresh! He makes them new!

We can speak worlds of meaning into existence, too, for our word is not altogether different from God's. *Our* word has power. *Our* word discloses who we are and gives evidence of those circumstances that are good or pleasing to us. What is good or pleasing to us, of course, may or may not be good or pleasing to God. But it can be made so and has been made so in Christ. In Christ, the world-creating Word of God resonates with the world-creating word of human beings. In him, the conflict between the two ceases, and there is peace. In him, the rich and poor, old and young rulers, give up their deathly intent to "go it alone"—to be the gods of God. Buechner calls that overcoming of human self-destructive pretension our homiletical "fairy tale," a fairy tale come true.[10] We really do have something to celebrate in Christ. We have the fact of our being "born again." We have the fact of our resurrection from the dead. After all, even as Christ is, so we are to be. Or, to reverse the poet's thought, not what we are, are we. Instead, we are what we are to become. We are eschatologically, not ontologically, determined. The future, *our* future, is fixed in Christ. As the theologians state it: In him God is present for us, and in him we are present for God.

That claiming of human life for God in Christ is always present in preaching. It always will be there, if what is going on is, in fact, preaching; and like everything else in preaching, because it is there, it will call for some sort of response from the preacher. Furthermore, that response will be indicated both in *what* the preacher says, and in *how* it is said. *What* the preacher says will evidence God's claim upon human life in terms of specific, or not so specific, issues, problems, or proffered courses of action—the exigences, as the rhetorician Lloyd Bitzer has called them, of any preaching situation.[11] *How* the preacher responds to God's claim upon human life—upon his or her own life, as well as upon the lives of others—will be evidenced, on the other hand, in the preacher's sense of purpose. Is it assured, tentative, happy, alarmed, excited, reserved, hopeful, or anguished? What is the overall "mood" of the sermon? Does it seem that something important is at stake, or that nothing is at stake? Is the preacher's affirmation tortured or joyous? We have considered the movement of thought in preaching and the specific contexts that give rise to any movement of thought. Now the time has come to deal with that which establishes overall mood. Every sermon expects something. The mood of any sermon, therefore, is determined by the response made to that expectation.

As I have indicated, the claim you are listening for and seeking to respond to in preaching is always present, but the impact of that claim upon the way people conduct their affairs, though also always

Richmond Hill Library
2209 East Grace Street
Richmond, VA 23223

present, can be either specific or nonspecific. The claim has to do with our being what and who we are, and Whose; the implications of that claim have to do with our actions. Thus being and doing—life and action—are held together.

Following are two excerpts from sermons, representing the two types of claim-implication pattern. In the first sermon, the implications are specific, as the claim is explicit. In the second, the implications of God's claim upon human life are nonspecific. Select one or both excerpts to study and practice aloud. Listen for the claim made upon you and for its possible or stated implications for engaging life. Then respond to the claim as felt and interpreted by you, trying to express that response—your basic attitude toward what is being said—through vocal and physical gesture. Record yourself, if possible on video tape, or at least on audio tape. When you play back the tape, remember to listen and/or to watch, not simply for movement of thought and empathic response to the context that gives rise to that movement of thought, but also for the basic or overall attitude that gives tone and sense of purpose to the sermon as a whole. After you have studied the tape, try to define in just a few words the overall attitude of the sermon as delivered by you. If you find that such definition is impossible, perhaps you had better "get into" the sermon again and give it another try. What you are doing here is not just an exercise in analyzing, interpreting, and speaking a sermon. You are learning to listen for the claim made upon people's lives by God in Jesus Chist. If you cannot hear and respond to the claim yourself and establish some sort of appropriate attitude toward it, the likelihood is that your listeners will not be able to hear and respond to it either. This is the preaching moment, and whatever of consequence is to happen, happens now, or it does not happen at all.

Claim Made with Specific Implications

The See-Saw View of Life

In his book of a few years back, *The Exurbanites*, A. C. Spectorsky offers this commentary on American manners: "On the New York Central's commuting train down the Harlem Valley there are still seats aplenty at Chappaqua, and the courtly, old-world grace with which women are permitted to climb on board first would delight the most captious. By the time the train arrives at Pleasantville, however, seats are scarcer and only the most attractive or the most decrepit women are given any priority. Come White Plains and women are thrust aside; every man for himself."

It is easy to be generous when there is enough to go around. But when supplies are limited it is quite a different matter. When there are three cars and only two parking places; five men wanting work and only four job openings; ten nations needing oil and only enough for nine—what then? It is in the crucible of scarcity that what we are and what we believe are most clearly revealed.

The specter of scarcity is beginning to impose its eerie presence on the American way of life. Ever since pilgrim days we have lived with the notion that our frontiers and resources were perpetually expandable. Settlers who couldn't make it in the east pushed on across the Alleghenies. Those who could not find land to their liking in Kansas could rig up their wagons and roll on to Oklahoma. Those whose prospects for the good life were stymied in Ohio could cross the Rockies to pan for gold or dig for silver.

The prodigality of nature was consistently assumed. If a man needed a house he chopped down enough trees to build one. When he was hungry he shot a buffalo or deer. If he dug for copper and exhausted a particular mine he would simply snap a lock on the front gate, pack up his gear, and go digging somewhere else. We were still at Chappaqua. There was plenty of room for all!

As industrialization set in, however, we began to feel the pinch of want, just a bit. Not having everything we needed we used our wealth to trade for vital resources. Every year this country imports more than fifteen billion dollars worth of goods—agricultural products, metals, and non-metallic minerals such as petroleum. The notion persisted that whether home-grown or imported we could get what we had to have. There was no reason other than mental stagnation or plain laziness why the Gross National Product could not go up, and up, and up each year! We were at Pleasantville now. Seats were not quite as plentiful as before, but if a man kept his wits and worked hard everything would be all right.

Now suddenly we are at White Plains! At the "every man for himself" stage. The frontiers are gone, geographically speaking. Much of nature that we ravaged en route to our prosperity has been rendered permanently sterile. Old sources of vital foods and minerals are drying up. Countries that were once willing to trade away precious commodities to us are beginning to have second thoughts. Enormous pressures are being exerted on the United States by members of the third world—Africans, Asians, South Americans; and impoverished blacks, whites, browns, reds and yellows of our own country. More and more people are wondering why those of us in North America who comprise but 20% of the world's population should consume 80% of the world's wealth.

. . . What is new in our situation is a growing awareness that we live in a finite universe. God is infinite, but the world is not. This has always been theoretically true, but now it is actually and existentially true. We live on a see-saw. If one is up too high, another must be down too low. Whether I intend it or not, my indulgence in luxury may deprive a brother of some necessity. Asking for seconds at the table is harmless enough. Unless, of course, you know of a neighbor who has not eaten for three days. And especially if that neighbor's toil has helped to set your table!

. . . What response *can* we make? What response *should* we make to all of this? . . . To be . . . specific, these suggestions. There are some assumptions or axioms that we Americans have been living on that must be reconsidered. . . .

I would suggest that we must re-open . . . such assumptions as: The unchecked expansion of national economies; the right of everybody to have as large a family as he wishes, the absolute value of human life over all other life.

But coming closer to home, there is something we can do as members of a given congregation. We can seek so to reorder our investments that the social betterment of men, rather than the highest monetary return, may govern what we do. . . .

But even closer to home as individual members of this body, I believe that given the crisis of mounting scarcity it is incumbent upon us that we consider a simpler style of life. . . .

I heard the other day over the radio, word that corporations are having a hard time getting executives to come to New York. It seems that New York City cannot provide them with the "amenities to which they have grown accustomed." This leads one to wonder what businessmen in France had the coziest amenities before the revolution.

It is so hard to come down once you have been up there. I interceded once for a man who was store manager for a nationwide chain. His salary was around the forty thousand a year mark. He had been weighed in the balance by top management and found wanting and was summarily fired. When I got to the president of the company I asked if my parishioner might be given another store to manage. The answer was "No, he doesn't have it." Could he not then be made a departmental manager in some other store? The answer was, "No. We've learned that psychologically this never works. Once you have been a manager you can't come down."

Is there no power in the Gospel? Is there no compulsion in the mercy of God? Is there no illumination in the model of Jesus himself that could make us willing to come down if perchance it would help others to come up? Besides, does it not belong to the wisdom of the Gospel to give what you cannot keep to gain what you cannot lose? . . . The see-saw is in effect. We may not be comfortable with this, but this is a fact of life. When someone is up too high, someone else is down too low. But with love, the love of God for us—his love in us, there is no see-saw model. The beauty of God's love is that the more it is lavished, the more it grows. The more we act on it the more we have. It is to this love that I ultimately appeal. I believe our country can do it. I believe this church can do it. I believe that severally and individually as members of this congregation we can do it. And I believe we should.[12]   (Ernest T. Campbell)

Claim Made with Nonspecific Implications

The Name of the Nameless

Then Jacob asked . . . "Tell me, I pray, your name?"
                                                   —Genesis 32:29

And you shall call his name Jesus, for he will save his people from
their sins.   —Matthew 1:21

We ask, "What's in a name?" We mean that there is nothing in
it. In truth there is little enough in our names, for they are hardly
more than tags by which the mailman brings Christmas presents
to our house instead of to some alien door. What, for instance,
could the name "Buttrick" mean? "George" means a farmer, as in
Vergil's *Georgics*, and I scarcely know the right end or wrong end
of a plow. But there was a time when names had meaning. . . .
The name, "John" once meant "gift of God," just as Joshua (Jesus)
once meant "savior." In times from which the book of Genesis is
drawn men believed that if they could learn the name of a god,
they would possess the god's very power; for a name then meant
almost a man's or a god's nature.
    All of which brings us to an eerie story in that same book of
Genesis. A man tried to cross a river at midnight, and the river-god
disputed the passage. This story, you can see, is as old as an early
polytheism. The man and the god wrestled, by the river churned
white, in the darkness. "What's your name?" asked the ghostly
adversary. "Jacob," answered the man. Now it was the man's turn:
"Tell me, I pray, your name." Oh, no! Learn the god's secret,
steal the god's power? Oh, no: gods are shrewder than men. So the
god answered: "Why do you ask after my name?" It was believed in
those days that gods feared the light, so the god soon exclaimed:
"Let me go, for the day breaks." Now the man had the advantage
as they wrestled in the slowly broadening light: "I will not let you
go unless you bless me." Thus the man prevailed to win the
blessing. A weird story . . . and you may well ask, "What has that
to do with Christmas?"
    It has this to do: God and we hold the same kind of
conversation. He asks, "What is your name?" We try to quip our
way out of it, saying airily, "What's in a name?" But name means
nature, and we begin to ask what our name really is—dust or
divinity, perverseness or child of eternity? Then God asks again,
"Where do you live?" We are about to answer, "That's a silly
question. It doesn't matter, does it? And in any event, You should

know." But the answer dies on our lips. Where *do* we live? Not on this little swinging ball called Earth, for we are always strangers in time and space. So we evade the question by turning it back on God: "Tell me, I pray, your name." If we only knew! Is the name, "Fear," an invisible shape that seizes us at midnight on the banks of the turbulent river called Time? . . . Or is the name, "Nothingness"? That would be a worse name than "Fear." Perhaps everything we say and do is an attempt, a groping question, to learn God's name. But since he is God and we are creatures of flesh, how can we ever know unless He tells us?

These questions bring us back to the man Jacob. He was afraid that the name of the river-god might be "Judgment." Twenty years earlier he had wronged his blind father and his casual brother to steal his brother's birthright. That is why his name was Jacob: "the supplanter." Meanwhile he had prospered. He was eager now, as he was returning home, that bygones should be bygones; but neither memory nor history was ready to help him. A dirty trick ought not to live any longer than a dog: it should die in twenty years. But in memory and history it refuses to die. Sometimes Jacob had regretted the deception, but usually he had been too busy to think about it. He had lived alternately by his wits and by his heart, like the rest of us; and like the rest of us, he had not been sure which was his name and nature. Now he had to know, for his brother, whom he had not seen for twenty years, was marching toward him with four hundred men. What *was* his own name—"Deception"? What was the god's name—"Nemesis"? This name business became momentous, there at midnight on the bank of an eerie stream.

Conscience is a strange affair. It gives different verdicts in different cultures, but moves through all cultures dividing right from wrong—and with some common judgments as, for instance, about a man's home and the worth of a man's life. It can be in error and needs repeated checking, as a compass needs it, but like a compass, it seems to move in obedience to a mysterious magnetic north. Our shallow modern theory reckons it a hang-over from a childhood fear of our parents, but that makes no sense, for even a child's conscience is sensitive both to his own sins and to parental cruelty. Our shallower theory reckons it a vestigial affair from ancient tribal custom or social convention. But why, then, does prophetic conscience convict both custom and convention, as in the instance of war or the "double standard"? Conscience can become psychotic, but that very fact implies a healthy conscience. . . . Therefore, we and all men wonder if the name of God is "Judgment"; and as with Jacob, we wonder with sufficient cause. . . .

Thus Jacob and his god. Thus we and God, God ever asking our name and we ever asking His name. The word "God" comes presumably from the root word for good. But how can that root word be squared with an earthquake or a maniac? Yet the pity in us which asks that question belongs somewhere within the good. Perhaps all the names we surmise about God are partly true. His name must be for us "Fear," for we think of Him with awe; and "Judgment," for if there were no judgment, man's life might become trivial; and "Beauty," for black branches against the snow at sunset almost grip a man's throat in their beauty; and "Truth," for scientists and witnesses at court must honor truth. The trouble is that we do not know the central and sovereign name. The trouble is that no list of abstract nouns can ever fill our longing, for we yearn to know that God is here where we live. Presumably He has a supernal name, but that name is beyond our ken; and we dare not, cannot, take it on our lips. Doesn't God have a human name?

Then Christmas in its gentleness: "You shall call his name Jesus, for he will save his people from their sins." The doubts at once come knocking at our door, but so lovely is the story, we wonder if we have any right to invite them. God revealed in a Babe in swaddling clothes—that is, with linen bands around the tiny shoulders and thighs? God thus made known? God disclosed as a Babe in a poor and inconspicuous home, a Babe who had a manger for his first cradle, with all kinds of strange people crowding in-between the camels and donkeys to look at him? If that be so, the doubts still thronging and knocking within us, God's name is "Lowliness" and "Emmanuel": "God with us." Perhaps we should doubt the doubts instead of giving them entrance. For this is true: if God had kept the whole heaven between us and Him, if always He had been only ultimate Truth, like snow on some inaccessible mountain, how would we know Him to be "good"? Or if He had come near as an angel, how could we have worshiped? What do angels know about human tears and laughter? If the name is "Jesus," we can account for the love in us, for our love might then be the broken image of His love. We could account also for the running fire of glory, beneath the deceit, in any Jacob. . . .

God has many names. . . . His name is "Mystery," for the heavens were not emptied when Jesus came; and if God were not Mystery, men could never have worshiped. His name is "Power": He lifts the cosmos and will not let the name of Jesus die. His name is "Judgment," for our life is not a jaunty affair in which Jacob-deceit goes unnoticed after twenty years, in which God casually wipes His lips of our wantonness, saying, "Oh, don't mention it"; life is a momentous once-for-all encounter. His name is "Holiness": people who glibly wish they might meet Jesus forget that once his friends cried out in agony: "Depart from me, for I am a sinful man, O Lord" [Luke 5:8]. His name is "Enigma": we simply cannot construe the plan which includes earthquakes and maniacs, and should not pretend that we can. But the central name, if only because it starts our tears and joy and deepest resolve, is Jesus: "for he will save his people from their sins." . . .

A large man on a plane said to me, "The name's Coulter, from Texas. What's your name?" I was mulling over this sermon and almost answered, "Jacob," and might have been right. Jesus meets us. "My name's Jesus. What's yours?" If we are wise, we shall say: "Jesus! Lord, that my sins may be forgiven!" At Christmas time God asks us our name. Then we can tell Him that our name is not now (not at Christmas time) "dust" or "pride"; for our name is now lost in the name of Jesus, and thus forever found. God asks us then: "Where do you live?" We can tell Him since it is Christmas, "I live at Harvard, in Cambridge, on the tiny ball called Earth, in a universe that goes clean beyond my mind. But not beyond Yours: I live in the Father's house because an Elder Brother has led me home." Everything good and joyous is in one name—the name of Jesus.[13] (George A. Buttrick)

V. THE PREACHER'S GOSPEL AND CONVERSATION IN PREACHING

Principle number four for the listening preacher: Listen for the explicit or implicit kerygma that gives coherence to the sermon as a whole and that sustains you in your effort to relate the world of religious experience evoked in scripture to the experience of people today.

In the previous chapter I spoke of both the world-creating Word of God and our own world-creating word being present and resonant in Christ. In Christ, the worlds that are good or pleasing to us are made good or pleasing to God. The enmity between human beings and God—between whole worlds of human life and God—is brought to an end, and there is peace. In Christ, there is no vain attempt to wrest lordship from God, but human life is rendered obedient to God. The life God would have us lead is revealed. All that we are and have is pressed into the service of what God would have us be and do. So we are claimed by God in Christ, personally and corporately; God makes us his own. Furthermore, that owning of us is accomplished *by* God and *for* God. We do not instance this reclamation; God does it himself. That is what grace means. What God intends for us he accomplishes among us, for his own sake, to "the praise of his glory." Not what we expect from God, but what he wills for himself and what he expects from *us* is disclosed in Christ. Our human story, the flow of our world-creating words, is disrupted, and new directions and new possibilities for ourselves and for other people, are given us. Our words "come a cropper" when they meet God's Word, and the moment for radical redefinition of who we are, where we are, where we came from, and where we are headed is upon us.[1] Our understanding of ourselves and our relationship to God, consequently, never is settled once and for all. Instead, that understanding always is being unsettled. Therefore, since preaching, by definition, evidences our attendance upon God's Word, it occasions our search for new words, for new *worlds* of meaning, being, and doing. We interpret our past afresh in the light of God's Word, grapple with the question of what it means to be faithful to God in the present, and search for the path to a more human and godly future. In preaching, to state it succinctly, we pursue a Christian interpretation of life.[2]

Our pursuit of that Christian interpretation rests upon biblical foundations that include both Old and New Testaments. Elizabeth Achtemeier, for instance, has indicated that the record kept for us in that collection of books called the Old Testament is of people who time and again had to rethink their understanding of God's promises and the nature of the fulfillment of those promises.[3] Understanding of God's formation of a nation through which all the families of the earth might "bless themselves" changed over the centuries and over the millenia. Understanding of the meaning of the Exodus from Egypt changed. Understanding of and implementation of the Law changed, commentaries upon it being written both in Hebrew characters upon parchment, and by successive generations of Israel's children, on battlefields, in towering and ruined temples, in synagogues, and on street corners. The warnings, hopes, and dreams of the prophets meant one thing to those who first heard them, and something else entirely to those who heard them anew in changed times and in different places. God's Word may have stood forever, but human understanding of it certainly did not! Just when Israel thought its mind was made up, something occurred that caused it to change: An enslavement took place or ended; a king was born or died; a prophet spoke or was silenced; a Christ was hailed, or rejected and killed. "You have heard that it was said to the men of old . . . but I say to you . . ." (Matt. 5:21-22). And so a New Testament was born, and the Word that was spoken and done by Christ had to be reckoned with again and again. A kerygma, or proclamation emerged over the years expressing who Christ was and what he meant to people; and that kerygma contained certain elements that the church felt were indispensable. Bruce Manning Metzger identified those elements as follows:

(1) The promises of God made in Old Testament days have now been fulfilled, and the Messiah has come:

(2) He is Jesus of Nazareth, who
    (a) Went about doing good and executing mighty works by the power of God;
    (b) Was crucified according to the purpose of God;
    (c) Was raised by God from the dead;
    (d) Is exalted by God and given the name "Lord";
    (e) Will come again for judgment and the restoration of all things.

(3) Therefore, all who hear the message should repent and be baptized.[4]

In different places, among different people, and at different times, however, certain aspects of the kerygma were emphasized, while other aspects were almost ignored. And at all times and in all places the elements in it received varying interpretations, according to the insights of individuals and groups who were determined to scrutinize and redirect their lives in light of it. They probed the possible meaning of Old Testament response to the Word in the light of the New Testament kerygma. Response to the Word recorded in the New Testament received similar treatment. And their activity of the moment likewise was reviewed, assessed, and carried out in response to elements in the kerygma that seemed to raise significant issues and to disclose opportunities for responsible, godly action. *The* kerygma thus became *their* kerygma, and the gospel a matter of their personal experience as well as a fact of history.

Such personalizing of the gospel also happens in preaching. The kerygma, the Old and New Testament passages and the history of their interpretation in the church—all these, of course, preachers study carefully and honestly, using any and all scholarly resources available; but part of being honest in our homiletical research is to admit that our work never is done with complete objectivity. We cannot leave who we are out of our study. We cannot ignore our purpose in dealing with biblical and theological materials, for our aim is to preach, and our research and reflection therefore must yield some sort of experience that can be shared. Our study has a homiletical intent. Also, in developing the sermon that emerges from our study, it is evident who we are, what biases we have relative to the kerygma, what personalizing of the gospel has taken place in us. Each of us moves back and forth between Bible times and the present moment, along a path shaped by our previous encounters with an understanding of the Word of God, which has claimed us for a life of obedience or responsiveness to God in Jesus Christ. The preaching moment, in other words, is not divorced from other moments that have shaped our understanding of who and Whose we are. It is a product of our biography, as much as it is a product of our critical theological and biblical reflection upon issues and conditions of human life. Consequently, it is a partial but not a comprehensive statement of the gospel. It offers a look into Old Testament, New Testament, and contemporary word-created worlds from the place where we stand now. That place may change. Certainly, if our desire is to be responsible—that is, responsive to God's ever-fresh and renewing Word—the place we stand in our understanding of the gospel and of its implications for the conduct of life always will be susceptible to change. Our preaching thus always will be conditional—a thing of the moment; it will not be unconditionally and eternally true. Preaching represents where we are today. Tomorrow, however, we very well may be standing somewhere else.[5]

The preaching moment thus has room in it for personal, unique, and perhaps even idiosyncratic perception.[6] Every sermon will disclose the mind of the preacher, his or her habits of thought concerning the gospel, the biblical materials that bear witness to it, and the current events within which the gospel's implications must be lived out. It is the shape of your thoughts evidenced in your sermons, in fact, that give your sermons specificity, a certain character and coherence; that sets them off as distinctive homiletical efforts. Your sermons are *yours* precisely because they bear the stamp of who you are and how you have come to respond to God's Word, as the Scriptures bear witness to it and as you engage it in the throng and press of daily life. Your sermons are yours because the kerygmatic elements present in them are there by your choice and because the gospel offered by you when you preach is *your* gospel. Furthermore, your sermons, precisely because they are *your* sermons, will offer a Christian interpretation of life that is partial, tentative, momentary, acceptable to some people, objectionable to others, and always subject to review. To listen for the explicit or implicit kerygma that gives coherence to your sermons, sustaining you in your efforts to relate the world of scriptural experience to present-day experience, therefore, is to keep constantly aware of who you are—and of who you are not; of how limited your perceptions can be; and of how much you are indebted to other preachers and to those present with you in your own moment of preaching for their help in making possible a response to the whole gospel among men and women today.[7] You cannot possibly preach responsibly on your own. Your preaching requires the witness of the entire church to save it from mere peculiarity. To preach effectively, you need the voices of the other preachers of the church sounding all about you, and you need the careful, critical listening of those who attend to what you say. Your listeners are a vital part of the preaching moment; their contribution to that moment is as significant as your own. As a matter of fact, if you will recall our earlier discussion, *you* really are a listener, speaking for no other reason than to facilitate the listening of others.

That being the case, it would seem appropriate that your style of sermon delivery be conversational.[8] The conversational style may be contrasted with the declamatory style. The declamatory style assumes that those doing the talking somehow are in possession of truths that their listeners, for one reason or another, do not possess; or perhaps declamatory speakers simply are thought to be adept at putting into words the ideas, attitudes, and convictions that the listeners are assumed to share—beliefs or responses to the Word of

God that are reckoned transparently "correct."[9] Declaimers, therefore, simply announce to people what they have on their minds. They talk *to* those gathered before them; they do not enter into conversation *with* them. Further, they usually can assume that they are fully understood, provided they use words that are part of their listeners' vocabularies and speak with clarity, for there is no peculiar point of view that needs explication; there is no personalized gospel of any kind that needs to be told; there is nothing unique, and therefore nothing startling or arguable or tentative about the speakers' insights into the implications of the gospel for the conduct of present-day life. The declamatory style can be impressive, dramatic, celebrative, and convincing, if it is employed with skill. However, it is a style totally inappropriate for use in the proclamation of the gospel.

In the preaching moment, there is room for personalization of the meaning of the gospel. There is space for, and expectation of, the explication of responsible, unique points of view. With the conversational style there is no assumption of "aesthetic distance" between speakers and listeners.[10] On the contrary, the speakers, as it were, stand *with* their listeners, receiving and responding to whatever it is they are met to consider. Speakers, of course, are free to express fully the nature of their response to the subject. They may make strong, declarative statements; they may attempt to set the mood of the conversation, suggesting how the things they have to say may be appropriately or inappropriately received. Preachers certainly will do these things, for their job is to lead people's listening. They are not invited to climb into pulpits simply for the purpose of being part of whatever it is that congregations may wish to do. But the conversational preacher will lead the listening with sensitivity to the fact that what is said may not immediately "ring true" among those who hear it, and as H. H. Farmer has put it so well, the preacher will leave the listeners free to respond on the basis of their *own* "insight and sense of the truth."[11]

To speak conversationally when you preach, then, first and probably most obviously, means that you will look at those with whom you are conversing. Of course you will not look at your listeners ceaselessly, for even in a purely interpersonal chat, that kind of unrelieved, direct contact could not be tolerated. The constant look generates self-consciousness and unnecessary discomfort. So if you are relentlessly "eyeball to eyeball," you soon will find people looking away. In preaching conversationally, you may look at your notes from time to time, or "listen" with your eyes for the sound of a thought, or visualize an idea, focusing on it by avoiding any direct connection with your listeners. However, when you do look at those who are attending to what you say, you indeed will *look* at them—see them, catch their eyes, take note of the expressions on their faces, observe the erectness of their posture or the slump of their shoulders! For listening preachers, fellow listeners are important as persons in their own right. The presence of the listeners, therefore, is noted, and they are made to feel that their presence counts. Even in large, crowded sanctuaries, do not rule out such a personal touch, for looking at *groups* of people and actually seeing those groups can create for them a feeling of being included fully and personally in what is going on.[12]

In addition to establishing direct eye contact with listeners, conversational preachers will speak with an inflectional pattern that evidences concern about thoughts and about how they are heard by those who must comprehend and react to them. Inflection simply is the movement of pitch or, in certain cases, lack of such movement, on a single syllable. In declamatory style, downward inflections usually will predominate, particularly on syllables at the ends of word groupings. To catch the feel of this manner of speaking, read aloud the following passage, using exclusively falling inflections at the ends of phrases. I have placed arrows to indicate the points of downward inflection.

Ask, and it will be given you; ↓ seek, and you will find; ↓ knock, and it will be opened to you. ↓ For everyone who asks ↓ receives, ↓ and he who seeks ↓ finds, ↓ and to him who knocks it will be opened. ↓

Pretty cut and dried, wasn't it? Nothing to think about there—just something to accept, more as fact than as experience. In the declamatory style, the listeners have the feeling that conclusions are being dished out to them. Reflection on what is said, weighing of thought, holding ideas in the mind to assess them, is not encouraged. The listeners, in other words, are treated as passive receptors—or worse yet, admirers, if the declamation is given with great skill. In the conversational style, however, people are encouraged to think about, to evaluate, to savor, and to accept or reject ideas. Their participation in the consideration of the preacher's thoughts is invited. Thus they may come to regard themselves as active participants in the preaching moment. Preachers who wish to speak conversationally, therefore, will use all the different types of inflection, changing pitch in such a way that the relationship between thoughts can be perceived easily. To be specific, besides downward inflections, there are rising, monotone, and circumflex inflections. Downward inflections imply assertiveness—declaration of the speaker's will—and suggest completion of thought. Rising inflections imply an attitude of questioning—deference to the will of the listener—and suggest incomplete thought. Circumflex inflection—movement of pitch up and down and perhaps up again, on a single syllable—suggests complexity of thought. And monotone inflection at the end of a phrase indicates that the thought just begun will be completed in a subsequent statement.[13] To experience these variances for yourself, try reading conversationally the passage from Matthew (7:7-8), which you delivered moments ago in declamatory fashion. As you do, remember to make use of all four types of inflection just described, and make sure that your inflectional pattern gives sound to the relationships that you see between phrases or word groupings.

There is one thing more that needs to be said about the conversational style in preaching, and that is that all those factors that contribute to responsible expression of thought and that were discussed in the previous chapters, still must come into play. Listening preachers, speaking conversationally, will attend to the movement of thought in preaching, noting the fulcrum or turning point, climax, and denouement of their sermons. They will speak their words with color, reacting empathically to the experiences that give rise to movement of thought evoked in their sermons. And they will establish the overall mood appropriate to what they have to say, by listening for and responding to the claim made upon them and upon their listeners when they preach. To do all that and, additionally, to establish a measure of direct contact with listeners, expressing thoughts in such a way that listeners may feel that they are being invited to consider and not merely to accept them, obviously will require careful, extensive preparation for the preaching moment. Conversational preaching, after all, does not just happen. It comes about through thoughtful practice and as a result of the confident self-control that thoughtful practice makes possible. That is not to say that there is no room in conversational preaching for response to what sometimes is called the inspiration of the moment. In fact, just the opposite is the case. The better prepared you are *for* the preaching moment, the more relaxed and spontaneously responsive you can be *in* it. Lack of sufficient preparation, on the other hand, very possibly can tie you in knots and so fill you with anxiety concerning where the next word is coming from and how it ought to be said, that response to ideas, images, attitudes, and convictions—genuine engagement of them—and alertness to listener reaction is all but impossible. Perhaps the following are paradoxical statements, but I feel your own observations, sooner or later, will confirm them: Those sermons that are most capable of adaptation to the requirements of the preaching moment have been prepared in the most detailed fashion; those sermons that appear most spontaneously delivered have been practiced conscientiously and thoroughly; and those sermons that seem to be most fresh and "first-timely" have taken on definitive shape in the preacher's mind.[14] I think Robert Frost's delightful bit of verse can be applied, without any hesitation, to preaching.

> Let chaos storm!
> Let cloud shapes swarm!
> I wait for form.[15]

Now without waiting *too* long for form, prepare a sermon of your own composition for delivery. Take note of the fulcrum of your text, the climax, and the denouement. Practice speaking the words with color, allowing yourself to enter empathically into the experiences your sermon is intended to evoke. Listen for the claim made upon you and your listeners in your sermon, also, as you ready it for presentation, and so respond to that claim that an overall mood appropriate to the preaching moment at hand may be discerned. Finally, as you preach your sermon to your homiletics class or similar group, be sure to establish direct contact with those listening to you. Look at them when it seems right to do so—*really* look at them—and speak your thoughts with inflectional variety, giving sound to the relationships between the phrases or groupings of words. Let your manner of delivery be such that your listeners may feel invited to consider what you have to say and to respond on the basis of their own insight and sense of the truth. If possible, use video tape, so that you have a record to consult in the process of evaluation.

VI. VOICE AND ARTICULATION FOR THE LISTENING PREACHER

Now that the principles of sermon delivery have been explored in detail, it would seem appropriate to deal, to some extent at least, with the subject of voice and articulation. The human voice, after all, is a primary instrument of expression in preaching. Through use of the voice, preachers evidence their attention to the movement of thought in their sermons; indicate empathic involvement with the contexts that give rise to that movement of thought; respond to the claim made upon them and upon their listeners, thereby establishing overall mood; and demonstrate their awareness of the personalization of the gospel, which inevitably occurs in all moments of proclamation and which gives such moments their uniqueness. Of course, an exhaustive discussion of the subject of voice and articulation is not possible here.[1] Furthermore, treatment in depth of specific individual voice and/or articulation faults, and programs of improvement, need to be carried out under the supervision of trained professionals. I might suggest, in passing, that more of that kind of intensive work needs to be done in our seminaries; but the best that can be hoped for at present is greater awareness of how voice is produced and how it can be used to express what is going on in a preacher's mind. There are three goals for this study of voice and articulation for the listening preacher: responsiveness, clarity, and variety.

DEVELOPING VOCAL RESPONSIVENESS

At the outset, it needs to be recognized that if your voice is to be responsive, it must have something to which it can respond—some demand needs to be placed upon it. What could be more self-evident? Yet, believe it or not, that obvious fact often is overlooked. Many times preachers' voices seem dull, dead, dry as dust, because the persons behind those voices are anything but alive to the preaching moment and to the demands it places upon them. They do not listen for the movement of their own thoughts; consequently, those thoughts seem leaden, immovable, and unmoving. They do not enter empathically into the situations of human life alluded to in their sermons; thus, even if those sermons are composed with concrete nouns and action verbs, and are chock-full of anecdotes, they seem abstract, impersonal, and irrelevant. If preachers do not let God's claim upon them and upon their listeners elicit from them some appropriate response, the resulting sermons sound uneventful—"underwhelming," as some wag has put it; nothing much seems to be at stake. Such sermons give the appearance of counting for nothing, and the preaching moment therefore seems to be devoid of mood and any sense of purpose. Finally, some preachers, some of the time—and maybe a few preachers, all the time—do not, as it were, reach out vocally and take hold of their listeners, inviting them to share in animated conversation. Perhaps they rely exclusively on sound amplification equipment to do their projecting for them. In any case, they speak without intensity. Their voices seem tired and sleep-filled, and their listeners, despite the audibility of the sermons, accordingly may be left with the impression that they are meant only to overhear what is being said, if they should happen to be inclined toward such eavesdropping. What is being said, in other words, does not sound as if it is the listeners' own immediate and crucial business. To deliver you from any possibility of speaking in such an unmotivated and unresponsive way, the principles of sermon delivery were discussed first in this book, and only now are issues of vocal technique and articulation being considered. Voice technique is developed in response to a technique of thought, for vocal responsiveness depends upon adequate mental demand.

Another contributing factor in vocal responsiveness is the

awareness that speech is a wholistic, physical act. It is not an act only of the mind and vocal mechanism; it involves a person's whole body, from toe tip to scalp. In any athletic event, certainly, the participant's whole person is involved, is it not? At the moment of the tip-off in a basketball game, for instance, every player on the court is attentive to the referee, to the ball, and to the two people jumping at center, as well as to the position and leaning of all the other players. Muscles are not tensed, but they do have tonicity, and they are quivering with impulse. Minds, arms, legs, hands, feet—all are alert, ready for split-second decision and action. If such is not the case with a particular player, usually that player, sooner or later, is singled out by the coach for reprimand. "Come on! Let's get into the game!" is what you will hear shouted. Likewise, performing artists—instrumentalists or vocalists—play and sing with their entire being. Watch the expressions on their faces and you will soon see that this is true. Their intention is to express the meaning of the music being performed, with every inch of their persons. No part of them is "out of it." On the contrary, every part of them is in it—or they will not be performing artists for very long! That is not to say they are "uptight." To the contrary, they are at ease—but they are not at rest! Their concentration is total, and they are ready and willing and able. And nothing less may be expected of a preacher! Preachers, of course, need not be athletic, and certainly they should not come to think of themselves as performing artists of the pulpit. That has been made clear in our discussion of the contrast between declamatory and conversational speaking styles and of the inappropriateness of the former to the preaching moment. Still, the preacher does need to respond to the demands of the preaching moment with body, as well as with mind and voice. If he or she does not, you can be assured that what the body is saying—or failing to say, through noninvolvement—is what will be "heard" by the listeners; and all the words might just as well go, literally, out the window. You can also be assured that the voice itself will not sound as clear and intense as it might. That fact was brought home to me more years ago than I care to remember when, as a high school youngster singing in a chorus, I slouched into a late afternoon rehearsal, physically ready for nothing so much as sleep. The same was true of most of those singing with me; and what our bodies felt, our voices reflected. Our director, nevertheless, snapped us to attention with a look and a commanding voice that brought us to the edge of our seats. "Sit up! Feet down flat on the floor! Look as though you are alive, and pretty soon you will sound it, and soon after that you will feel it." We did what she said; and no sooner had we, than we found she was right. A responsive voice is part of—not separate from—a responsive body. And that is just as true for preachers as for singers.

Yet more specifically than is the case for mental concentration and total physical involvement, vocal responsiveness in preaching depends upon an adequate supply of breath, efficiently used. In breathing for life, as opposed to breathing for speech, you will note that there is rhythmical inhalation and exhalation. In other words, the time spent breathing in and breathing out is very nearly the same, regardless of degree of physical exertion. In speaking, however, the breath is taken in swiftly, but as a rule, it is let out slowly, sustaining vocalization and accommodating the outflow of air to the pattern of speech. The question, therefore, is how to control that sustained exhalation of air. It is recommended now by nearly all reputable voice teachers that the locus of control should be the muscles of the abdominal wall and the lower rib cage. At one time, upper chest activity and the raising and lowering of the clavicles (shoulder blades) sometimes was encouraged. The upper chest, however, is the least expandable portion of the thoracic cavity. Consequently, the attempt to raise and expand it in inhalation does not provide as adequate a supply of air to the lungs as might be obtained in other ways. Also attempted control of exhalation through collapse of the rib cage and dropping of the shoulders is often far from efficient. Such control is sometimes accompanied by excessive tension in the muscles of the larynx or voice box and in the vocal folds or bands themselves.[2] The result is what often has been referred to as "tight" voice. More will be said about that later when phonation or initiation of sound is discussed. For the present, suffice it to say that upper chest or clavicular breathing is not encouraged.

Instead, abdominal breathing is recommended. Abdominal

breathing is natural breathing and is usually involuntary. In inhalation, the muscles of the abdominal wall relax, as the diaphragm, a muscular "floor" separating the thoracic cavity above it from the abdominal cavity, contracts. In exhalation, on the other hand, the muscles of the abdominal wall tighten slightly, while the diaphragm relaxes. The lowering and raising, tightening and relaxing of the diaphragm increases and decreases the size of the thorax, thus allowing the lungs to receive and release air. When the movement of the abdominal wall, in concert with the diaphragm, becomes conscious and voluntary, breathing for speech is made possible. Control can be sensed very readily, and the locus of control, being physically distant from the larynx, minimizes the possibility of hypertension in the initiation of sound. To experience the movement of the abdominal wall, lean back in the chair in which you are sitting and spread your hands across your abdomen. Relax, listen to your breath, and watch your abdomen and hands rise and fall as you take in and expel air. After several seconds, hold your breath for a moment, and then release it with a conscious tug of the abdominal muscles, particularly the lower abdominal and visceral muscles, as you say aloud, "wow." Do that at first rather quietly. Then increase the power of the tug and the volume of the "wow" until it is as loud as possible without vocal strain and without distortion of the vowel sound.

To gain further control of the exhalation of air and to relate it to phrasing, establish a strong, steady pull of the abdominal muscles and count slowly to ten. Then relax the abdominal wall, take in air, and repeat, counting this time to five. Once more, despite the fact that you probably are not nearly out of breath, relax the abdomen, replenish your reserve of air, and count slowly to ten again. Stand up and try the exercise still another time; on this "go 'round," place a hand on each side of your lower rib cage. Try to keep the rib cage flared as you pull with the abdominal muscles. This exercise should give you a very keen sense of control over your exhalation of breath.

Another factor in vocal responsiveness is phonation. Phonation has to do with the way in which sound is made. Frankly, it still is, to some extent, a mystery, but this much is known: If your larynx or "voice box," located at the top of your trachea or "wind pipe," is healthy, you can make sound.[3] That is because, by nature, the intrinsic muscles of your larynx are responsive to your thoughts. The least command from your brain literally nerves them for action. They tense and move the arytenoid cartilage, to which the vocal folds are attached at the back of the larynx, and so play a major role in determining the position of the vocal folds relative to each other and the degree of tension in them. When the vocal folds are separated in roughly a V shape and relaxed, air passes up from the lungs, through the trachea and glottis—the space between the vocal folds—noiselessly, as a rule, and with almost no resistance. When the vocal folds are tensed and brought into close proximity, narrowing or nearly closing the glottis, however, air coming up from the lungs through the glottis causes the vocal folds to flutter. Thus sound is initiated. The more tense the vocal folds, the higher the frequency of vibration and the higher the pitch. Conversely, the more lax the vocal folds, the lower the frequency of vibration and the lower the pitch. Let me repeat: The voice box, the muscles of the larynx, the vocal folds—all are naturally responsive to your thoughts. Therefore, you do not need to do anything consciously with the muscles of the throat, particularly the extrinsic muscles of the larynx, to initiate sound. In fact, any such direct, conscious attempt at manipulation only causes difficulties in phonation, general tightness, and/or "glottal attack."

Glottal attack refers to a faint cough-like explosion on the initiation of vowel sounds, due to excessive tension in the vocal folds as they come together, narrowing the glottis. General tightness is an annoying continuous stridency of tone, due to sustained excessive tension in the muscles of the larynx and vocal folds. To determine if you are utilizing the extrinsic muscles of the larynx so as to create greater tension in the laryngeal area than is needed for vocalization, place your hand on your throat in the vicinity of your Adam's apple, with the thumb and fingers pointing toward the hinges of your jaw. Swallow, and you will notice very definite external laryngeal muscle tension. That tension must be there when you swallow, but it should not be there when you speak or sing. Therefore, place your hand on your throat again and say, as you would for the doctor, "ahhh. . . ." If you feel no tension, fine. If you do feel some tense muscularization and movement, try saying "ahhh . . ." again, this time concentrating on relaxing the muscles of your throat. Also, if you hear that cough-like explosion of sound called glottal attack, try putting an "h" in front of the "ah" vowel. Establish a free attack and then attempt to keep that freedom after you have removed the "h." Here are some words that you might use in listening for hypertension in phonation, and especially for glottal attack.

Exercise for Discernment of
Glottal Attack and Hypertension in the Larynx

elm	apple	arbor	inch	eve
elegant	ample	arch	implicit	evening
emerald	apt	alms	impish	easy
errand	amble	Amish	itch	erasure

The opposite of hypertension—extreme laxness—may be present, with resultant breathiness. Just as the overtense voice is not free to respond adequately to thought, breathiness also limits vocal responsiveness. If you are breathy, your vocal folds simply are not approximating, or coming together as they should. More breath than is necessary for making sound is expelled, and a light, feathery tone results. The answer, of course, is not to tense the extrinsic muscles of the throat. That simply would introduce the problem just discussed. The answer, instead, is to listen closely to the sound you make and to expect something in it other than feathery lightness. You might also try placing the back of your hand a few inches in front of your mouth as you say "All's well that ends well."[4] There are few aspirated sounds in that sentence, and many of the final consonants are voiced continuants—"z" sounds in "all's" and "ends," and the "l" sound in "well." So if you feel much breath consistently on the back of your hand as you speak that sentence, you are breathy indeed. In fact, you should feel no breath, except from the "w" sound at the beginning of each "well" and the "th" sound in "that." To correct the problem, practice saying the sentence as previously described, until nearly all sensation of air on your hand ceases and the sound is fully vocalized. Think efficiency in the use of your breath. In other words, do not use more breath than you need for the sound you are making, for if you do, you are wasting it.

If your voice is to be responsive to your thoughts when you preach, it also is important to strive for what has been called balanced resonance. Balanced resonance simply means that you have appropriate reinforcement of the sound initiated by the vocal folds in your voice's primary resonators: the larynx, the pharynx, the mouth, and the nose. We have indicated that the larynx does its best work when there is no conscious effort on the part of the speaker to manipulate it. The pharynx (the upper throat extending from the top of the larynx to the rear of the mouth [oropharynx] and the nose [nasopharynx]) also does its work of sound reinforcement when it is relaxed and open. The length of the pharynx can be extended or shortened by lowering or raising the soft palate—the soft tissue at the rear of the mouth. When the palate is lowered, vocalized breath is admitted into the nasopharynx and nasal passages and is emitted through the nose, for production of the nasal consonants "m," "n," and "ng." In all other sounds in the English language, the soft palate is elevated and vocalized breath is emitted through the mouth.

The mouth or oral cavity obviously is the most modifiable of the primary resonators. The lips, tongue, soft palate, jaws—and therefore the cheeks—can be moved; and, as I am sure must be clear to you, they must be moved in order to articulate the various vowel, diphthong, and consonant sounds. (For convenience, I will use the term "vowel sounds" to refer to either vowels or diphthongs, or both.) Imbalance in resonance thus usually is associated with some sort of inappropriate oral activity. For example, if the jaw is opened and closed with excessive tension and muscularization for purposes of shaping the various sounds, the pharynx or upper throat, and perhaps the larynx, inherit a measure of tension also. The result is either a tense, thick, throaty tone or a tight, thin quality. In part, the problem can be resolved through modification of the articulation of specific vowels, a process that will be described in detail later in this chapter. The situation also can be corrected somewhat, however, by concentration upon relaxation of the jaw and throat muscles as vocalization takes

place. If you do have pharyngeal hypertension and hypertension in
the jaw as you speak, try gently pushing in with your fingers on the
hinges of your jaw as you think relaxation, and vocalize these sounds
in connected sequence: ah—ay—ee—oh—oo. As you do the
exercise, listen carefully. Your voice, after all, not only should *feel* as
free and open as possible, but it should *sound* that way, too.

It ought to sound free of hyper- and hyponasality as well, for those
conditions also create an imbalance in resonance, which can limit
responsiveness of the voice to the need for full expression of thought
and feeling. Hyponasality is insufficient nasal reinforcement of
sound and is most obvious in production of the nasal consonants
"m," "n," and "ng." But it also has an effect on the production of
vowel sounds, which should have some indirect nasal resonance,
but no direct flow of vocalized breath into the nasal passages, or
emission of that breath through those passages. For example, the
vowel sounds in words such as *men, man, mean, mine, moan,
moon,* and *main,* inevitably are affected by the nasal consonants that
precede or follow them. Though the vowel sounds are not to be fully
nasalized, there should be a certain minimal nasal coloring as they
are blended into the flow of speech. Further, all vowel sounds should
have a certain brightness—even brilliance—which appropriate nasal
reinforcement provides. If that brilliance or bright, ringing, quality
is missing in your voice, try this exercise. Say—almost sing, if
possible—the phrase "sing——ah," being sure to stretch out the
"ih" sound of sing, and also the "ng" sound. Then snap the tongue
vigorously away from the palate or roof of your mouth as you finish
the elongated "ng" sound; concentrate on the feel of the palate lifting
away from the tongue and shutting off the passageway into the
nasopharynx. At the same time, however, attempt to carry over into
the vowel "ah" that ringing quality you heard and felt in producing
the "ng." Repeat the exercise several times, changing the vowel
sound successively to "ay," "ee," "oh," and "oo." Be especially alert
to the auditory, kinesthetic, and tactile sensations, for these are
indispensable in the process of achieving balanced resonance; and
balanced resonance is what you are after.

Resonance can be thrown off-balance, however, by hyper- as well
as by hyponasality. Hypernasality is excessive nasal resonance on

vowels and diphthongs. It usually is characterized not only by nasal reinforcement of sound, but also by some nasal emission. If hyponasality is speech that seems to be articulated with a stuffed nose, hypernasality is speech that always seems to be coming through the nose. It can be caused by a lazy palate that simply does not rise to shut off the access of vocalized breath to the nasopharynx and nasal passages as vowels and diphthongs are produced. If such laziness in the palate is the cause, the problem can be addressed by more vigorous articulation. Move the tongue, jaw, and lips with strength and energy as you carve all sounds—vowels, diphthongs, and consonants—and I think you will find that as other agents of articulation receive a more strenuous workout, the soft palate probably will become activated also. Hypernasality can be caused also by excessive tension in soft-palatal movement. The auditory sensation this produces is of a harsh, twanging quality. Such strident nasality is associated with overly vigorous and tense articulation. Therefore, the remedy is not to further activate the agents of articulation, but to relax them. Slowing the rate of speech and lengthening vowel sounds also may help. Finally, there is a type of hypernasality that results from too much nasal coloring of the vowels and diphthongs that are in close proximity to nasal consonants. This is called assimilative nasality. For instance, in saying the word "ban," if you anticipate the upcoming "n" as you are phonating the vowel, you may relax the soft palate too soon, resulting in partial nasal emisson of the vowel. Or if you carry over a nasal sound into the vowel or diphthong following it, you likewise may produce vowel or diphthong distortion. To deal with the problem, try saying the following word combinations in sequence, each time lengthening the continuent consonants, especially the nasal consonants, and the vowels or diphthongs. Also, carefully monitor your vowel sounds in each combination, for the production of the vowels and diphthongs should be kept consistent.

Exercise to Correct Assimilative Nasality

say-sane	fee-fiend	cry-crime	toe-tone	root-room
bay-bain	tea-team	tie-time	so-sewn	boot-boon
may-main	me-mean	my-mine	mow-moan	moo-moon

DEVELOPING CLARITY IN VOICE AND SPEECH

In addition to developing a voice that is responsive to your thought and feeling in preaching, it is important to strive for clarity; and clarity comes as a result of precise articulation of vowels, diphthongs, and consonants. It obviously would be totally beyond the scope of this book to go into a detailed explanation of the manner of articulation of each sound of the English language, identifying the most troublesome sounds and combinations of sounds and presenting corrective exercises. Still, certain general principles of articulation can be stated and illustrated, and the contribution of precise articulation to the processes of phonation and resonance can be indicated. First and most important—clarity of articulation begins with clarity of thought. That means not only that ideas and images need to be perceived clearly; it means also that the manner of expression of those ideas and images must be conceived definitely. Stumbling, halting, halfhearted articulation often is related to the "I know what I want to say, but I just can't figure out how to say it" syndrome. When it comes to preaching, at least, if you can't figure it out, it might be best not to attempt to say it. There is a certain eloquence in silence, and often there is warrant for it. Preachers need not ever be afraid of silence, in fact, for listeners, I am sure, appreciate inexpressible thoughts most if they are kept unexpressed until a way to communicate them with clarity has been determined.

Even after a way to phrase a thought has been found, however, you do not need to hurry into voicing it, for launching forth into expression of a thought before *you* are as ready as the thought is, also can cause stumbling. Hold ideas and images, once you have them. Let them work on you, and you on them, until you absolutely must come out with them. Seldom are listeners anxious to move preachers from thought to thought or from silence to sound. Most often it is just the other way around; preachers seem anxious to move themselves along. As W. J. Beeners has said, however, "the secret of poise is pause." When you need a pause, for example, because a thought is complicated or of great significance, take that pause. That moment will help you clarify what is on your mind, determine how your thought might best be expressed, and allow you to prepare yourself for expressing it. The result of such patience will be better articulation for you and better understanding for your listeners.

Another general principle of articulation is that the active agents of articulation—the lips, the tongue, and the soft palate—need to be capable of facile movement, if sounds are to be clearly formed and blended into words, phrases, and even larger units of thought. Also, the jaw always must be able to move freely and at times, vigorously. It may seem surprising even to mention something so obvious as the need for jaw movement, but the fact is that a good many people have developed the habit of barely moving their jaws when they speak. From the eyes down, their faces seem permanently set. The result is that most of the open vowel sounds are at least somewhat distorted. Further, when the jaw moves very little, facile movement of the agents of articulation often seems to be inhibited. Consequently, certain consonants may be sounded improperly, and combinations of sounds may be blurred. That one's facial expression is adversely affected by the immobile jaw, goes without saying, but that is another matter. For now, let it suffice to say that if articulation is to be crisp and clear, the jaw must move—not with tension, but with vigor—and the lips must be flexible and the tongue facile. An exercise that may be useful to you in loosening the jaw and activating the agents of articulation follows. Say the syllables aloud very slowly at first, connecting each successive sound to the one preceding it, but without blurring any sounds, and *exaggerate* the jaw, lip, and tongue movements. Then gradually increase the speed with which you make the sounds until you are talking as fast as you possibly can without vowel distortion and without stumbling on any of the consonants. Be sure to listen for clarity in every sound and for careful blending of sounds. Also, feel the movement of the jaw—its wide openness on "lah," its near closure on "lee." Feel the lip movement, too, especially the rounding on the vowel sound in "loh" and the rounding and greater protrusion on the "oo" in "loo." Hear the stop and plosion with voicing of the "b," the stop and voiceless plosion of the "p," and note the continuent, liquid quality of the "l." In other words, be totally aware of your facial and articulatory activity—listen to the sound, and feel it. Repeat the syllables at

least ten times in succession, increasing the rate of delivery with each
repetition.

Exercise for Jaw, Lip, and Tongue Movement

lah—— bay—— lee—— poh—— loo

In addition to the general principles of articulation just
explored, I would like to discuss the benefits precise articulation
can have for improved phonation and resonance and, consequently, for voice quality. The role that an understanding of the
process of articulation of vowel sounds—both vowels and
consonants—can play in influencing voice quality will be
considered first.

Perhaps you have heard a speech or voice instructor say that
someone's voice sounded "heavy," "too dark," or "muddy" and
that what was needed in order to "lighten" or "brighten" or "clean
up" the sound was "forward placing," getting sounds "out front,"
or "out of the throat." Or by way of contrast, you may have heard
that some voice was described as "thin," or "overly bright," or "too
light." Often when such terms are used to describe voice quality,
there is a need for "coloring," or "shading," of vowel sounds, so
that the heaviness or darkness or thinness or excessive brightness
may be overcome; and shading or coloring of vowel sounds is a
matter of articulation.

As I am sure you are aware, all vowels and diphthongs are
articulated in the mouth. Further, the place and manner of
articulation can be described in terms of tongue position, degree of
tenseness or laxness in the tongue, and lip movement—that is,
whether or not there is lip rounding.[5] To illustrate the use of the
tongue in the articulation of vowel sounds, consider the position of
the tongue in the production of the sound "ee," as in "see." The
tongue, you will note, is somewhat tense, and the *front* of the
tongue—not the tip—is elevated to the front of the roof of the
mouth. In production of the vowel sound "ah," as in "father," on
the other hand, the tongue lies flat and lax and is slightly retracted.
The vowel sound "ee," therefore, may be described as a high,

front, tense vowel, while "ah" is low, lax, and back. All the vowel sounds we customarily use can be described in terms of tenseness or laxness, highness or lowness of the tongue, and in terms of location—front or back. In the following diagram of vowel sounds, I have used phonetic symbols for the sake of convenience, but a listing of key words has been given also, so that you should have no difficulty understanding which vowel sound is represented by any given phonetic character. Notice that the highest, most tense, and most forward vowel sound is "ee," while the most lax front vowel is the "a" sound in words such as "hat." The most lax, low, back vowel sound is "ah," and the most tense, high, back vowel sound is "oo," as in "boot." Starting at top left with the "ee" sound, work your way down the front of the vowel chart and notice the gradual relaxing and retracting of the tongue. Then notice the slight tensing of the tongue again as you move up the back of the chart.[6]

Vowel Chart

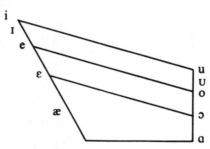

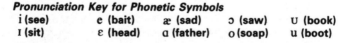

Pronunciation Key for Phonetic Symbols

i (see)	e (bait)	æ (sad)	ɔ (saw)	ʊ (book)
ɪ (sit)	ɛ (head)	ɑ (father)	o (soap)	u (boot)

If your tendency is to have a too consistently dark or heavy voice quality, you probably are shading the high, front vowels down and back. You also may be shading the back vowel sounds even farther back, retracting and tensing the tongue more than necessary. To brighten voice quality and to achieve forward placing, you need to raise and bring forward many—probably most—of your vowel sounds. The way to do that is to shade the vowel sound in the word "sit," for example, more in the direction of "ee" than in the direction of the sound you would find in "bait." Similarly, you would shade all other front vowel sounds up toward the sound above them, rather than toward the sound below them; and all back vowel sounds would be shaded forward, with as little tension in the tongue as possible. Thus, modifying your articulation of vowel sounds will effectively modify voice quality, brightening the dark tones and making the heavy tones lighter. Obviously, the process can work conversely, too, allowing you to darken, or to make more "substantial," any overly bright or thin tones. It is important to realize that no two people make vowel sounds in exactly the same way, with exactly the same forwardness or tenseness or laxness. In other words, everybody always does some shading. You should become familiar enough with your own voice to determine if any habitual shading or coloring patterns will so limit your voice quality that you cannot fully express various shades of meaning—the lightness or heaviness, for instance, of an idea or image. After all, we are not interested merely in producing pear-shaped tones, but in achieving the flexibility that will allow us to express the quality of our thoughts clearly.

Clear articulation of consonants also can play a role in general voice improvement. Correct articulation of voiced consonants, and especially voiced continuents, can aid with control of breath, resonance, and projection. The way in which the nasals "m," "n," and "ng" can contribute to a ringing quality in vowel sounds has been discussed. In addition to those voiced, nasal continuents, however, there are a number of other resonant consonants, and audible, clear speech certainly is made more probable if those consonant sounds are properly produced. The following is a listing, in voiced and voiceless pairs, of all the consonants used in the English language. Read through the list pair by pair and notice how much more breath is used in articulating voiceless consonants—consonants formed without vocal-fold participation—than in articulating consonants that are voiced, that have vocal-fold involvement, and that are resonant.

The Consonants of English: Voiceless and Voiced Pairs

	Voiceless	Voiced	
	p	b	
	t	d	
	k	g	
Nasal sounds have no voiceless counterparts.		m	
		n	
		ng	
	f	v	
("th" as in "thing")	th	th	("th" as in "this")
	s	z	
	sh	zh	("s" as in "vision")
	h		The "h" sound has no voiced counterpart.
("ch" as in "church")	tsh	dzh	("j" as in "judge")
The "l" sound has no voiceless counterpart.		l	
("wh" as in "when")	hw	w	
The "y" and "r" sounds have no voiceless counterparts.		y	
		r	

If you have a tendency to carry over the aspiration of voiceless consonants into vowel sounds, the result is more breathy, less resonant speech. "Devoicing" or "unvoicing" of voiced consonants likewise is indicative of a tendency toward breathiness; and of course, the more breathy and less resonant your voice, the less carrying power it has. If, on the other hand, you do not allow the aspirant quality of certain consonants to influence your production of vowel sounds, and if you are careful to give full vocalization to voiced consonants such as "z" and "zh" and "v," the result will be more resonant speech and a voice that carries, or projects, with greater ease. Always the aim is to control breath—to use it, not to waste it—and to be heard and understood with as little effort as possible.

To assist you in understanding whether a consonant should be voiced or voiceless—for spelling is not always a reliable indicator, since letters of the alphabet are not consistently phonetically descriptive—the following rule is helpful: *Paired consonants in a single syllable are both either voiced or voiceless, as determined by the first consonant of the pair.* For example, in the word "birds," the "d" and the "s" are paired in the same syllable. Since the first consonant of the pair, the "d," is naturally voiced, the second consonant, the "s," should be sounded as a "z," and the word is pronounced as though it were spelled "birdz." Similarly, the "r" and the "s" in the word "cars" are paired in a single syllable. The "s," therefore, again sounds as though it were a "z." Thus, despite its spelling, the word "cars" is not pronounced with an "s" sound at the end of it, but with a "z." The following exercise contains a number of voiced stop and continuent consonants, especially at the ends of words. Speak the sentences with full voicing of those consonants that should have vocal-fold participation and resonation and hear the strength that such care in articulation provides for your effort. Then for fun, and for contrast, you might try reading the exercise and intentionally devoicing, or even totally unvoicing, the final voiced consonants. I think you will hear readily how such a practice weakens the sound of your voice and reduces your capacity to project with ease. By the way, you should note that the letter "s," following a vowel in the same syllable, almost always is pronounced as a "z."

Exercise for Discrimination
Between Voiced and Voiceless Consonants

A. There is no news that is good news these days.

B. He was full of vim, vigor, and vitality, and so was she.

C. Judge me, my fellow citizens, not according to my words only, but according to my deeds.

D. Hamlet: His beard was grizzled—no?
   Horatio: It was, as I have seen it in his life,
              A sable silver'd.[7]

E. Everyone then who hears these words of mine and does them will be like a wise man who built his house upon the rock; and the rain fell, and the floods came, and the winds blew and beat upon that house, but it did not fall, because it had been founded on the rock. And every one who hears these words of mine and does not do them will be like a foolish man who built his house upon the sand; and the rain fell, and the floods came, and the winds blew and beat against that house, and it fell; and great was the fall of it.[8]

. . .

As with every other rule of the English language, so with the rule regarding voicing or unvoicing of paired consonants in a syllable; there are exceptions to prove it. Did you notice the exception in the paragraph you just read? It was the word "built." Obviously the "l" of that word is voiced; still, the final "t" remains unvoiced. In fact, under no circumstance I know, could a "t" or a "p" or a "k" ever become voiced. Yet their voiced counterparts, the "d," "b," and "g" can become unvoiced when coupled with a voiceless consonant in a single syllable—for example, "asked." In that word, the "e" is silent; thus the normally voiced "d" is paired with the "k" and is spoken as "t." So is the English language consistently anomalous!

VOCAL VARIETY—EXERCISES

The final section of this chapter on voice and articulation for the listening preacher is simply a series of exercises meant to help you experience the ways in which a clear and responsive voice can express the characteristics of various kinds of thought.

Throughout this chapter our concern has been not to develop beautiful voices, though ugly ones, I suppose, ought to be discouraged; nor has our concern been to stamp out regionalisms, though if someone's speech is so parochial that it cannot be understood by any except a small segment of the population, that ought to be looked into also. Rather, our concern has been to become aware that voice and articulation processes are vital to the full expression of whatever it is that people, especially preachers, may have on their minds and hearts. Voices need to be responsive to the textures and qualities of thoughts, if those thoughts are to be spoken in completeness. And clarity in speech is required so that ideas and images may be communicated and understood. The voice and articulation of the listening preacher, that is to say, should be of service in enabling the listening of others. They should be as disciplined as is the preacher's mind to the demands of the preaching moment. These exercises therefore, call for variety in voice quality, duration or rate, pitch, and volume. Study them, and when you feel that you are as ready as they are for expression, speak them aloud, giving appropriate vocal response to the ideas and images they contain.

Exercises in Voice Quality

O for a muse of fire, that would ascend
The brightest heaven of invention!
A kingdom for a stage, princes to act,
And monarchs to behold the swelling scene!
Then should the warlike Harry, like himself,
Assume the port of Mars; and at his heels,
Leash'd in like hounds, should famine, sword,
    and fire,
Crouch for employment.[9]

. . .

This bird died flying,
And fell in flowers.
Oh, what a world
Went with him. Ours.[10]

. . .

The sea is calm tonight.
The tide is full, the moon lies fair
Upon the straits;—on the French coast the light
Gleams and is gone; the cliffs of England stand,
Glimmering and vast, out in the tranquil bay.[11]

Exercises in Duration

I've known rivers:

I've known rivers ancient as the world and older than the
    flow of human blood in human veins.

My soul has grown deep like the rivers.[12]

. . .

Its quick soft silver bell beating, beating
And down the dark one ruby flare
Pulsing out red light like an artery,
The ambulance at top speed floating down
Past beacons and illuminated clocks
Wings in a heavy curve, dips down,
And breaks speed, entering the crowd.

The doors leap open, emptying light.
Stretchers are laid out, the mangled lifted
And stowed into the little hospital.
Then the bell, breaking the hush, tolls once,
And the ambulance with its terrible cargo
Rocking, slightly rocking, moves away,
As the doors, an afterthought, are closed.[13]

Exercises in Pitch

My long two-pointed ladder's sticking through a tree
Toward heaven still,
And there's a barrel that I didn't fill
Beside it, and there may be two or three
Apples I didn't pick upon some bough.
But I am done with apple-picking now.[14]

. . .

Who is here so base that would be a bondman?
If any, speak; for him have I offended. Who
is here so rude that would not be a Roman?
If any, speak; for him have I offended. Who
is here so vile that will not love his country?
If any, speak; for him have I offended. I
pause for a reply.[15]

Exercises in Volume

Now the Philistines gathered their armies for battle. . . . And
there came out from the camp of the Philistines a champion
named Goliath, of Gath, whose height was six cubits and a
span. . . . He stood and shouted to the ranks of Israel, "Why have
you come out to draw up for battle? Am I not a Philistine, and are
you not servants of Saul? Choose a man for yourselves, and let
him come down to me. If he is able to fight with me and kill me,

then we will be your servants; but if I prevail against him and kill him, then you shall be our servants and serve us." And the Philistine said, "I defy the ranks of Israel this day; give me a man, that we may fight together."[16]

. . .

> Here a pretty baby lies
> Sung asleep with lullabies:
> Pray be silent, and not stir
> Th' easy earth that covers her.[17]

. . .

Be still, and know that I am God.[18]

VII. THE LISTENING PREACHER'S BODY TALK

Voice is one of the primary instruments of expression in preaching; but obviously, it is not the only instrument of expression. Besides voice talk, there is body talk, and our discussion of the preaching moment would not be complete if we failed to give it due consideration. We are continually talking with our bodies, whether we are in pulpits or in pews, in automobiles or in conference rooms, at desks, at tables, at work, at play. You are talking with your body now, and if I could see you, I very possibly could "hear" a good deal of what you are saying. What was that? Did you indicate with a glance away from the page that you want to hold for a moment some thought that has occurred to you? Or did someone just step into the room and draw your attention? Maybe you are hunched over this book in a library cubicle, intent. Or perhaps you are leaning back in an easy chair, the book in one hand, your cooling cup of coffee in the other, relaxed—nothing too heavy to grapple with here. Maybe you are smiling now, enjoying just a little the bit of conversation I am trying to strike up with you. Or on the other hand, you may be thoroughly annoyed with this direct mode of discourse and anxious to have me give it up. However you are reading these words, and however you may be reacting to them, or failing to react, this much is certain: You are speaking loudly and clearly—voicelessly, but as surely as, with pen and ink, I am talking to you. Our bodies speak, and there is no way we can keep them quiet. Even our willed silence gives them something to say.

The task of listening preachers, therefore, is to say something with their bodies appropriate to the words they are speaking and to their purpose in speaking them. We have mentioned for instance, that to say our words with color necessitates not only vocal control, but conscious control of the body, as well. It is not the prerogative of preachers simply to let their bodies "do their own thing" when they preach. Instead, preachers are charged with the responsibility of representing their thoughts and their honest responses to those thoughts as faithfully as possible, through the use of both their voices and their bodies. When what is said with the body fails to correspond to what is said with the voice, or when bodily expression flagrantly contradicts verbal and tonal messages, confusion reigns, and listeners may be at a loss to determine just what is meant.[1] The communication channel becomes "noisy," you might say.[2] Or, to use a common metaphor, it seemingly may become charged with static. All of us have been on the receiving end of such conflicting messages, and so are aware of how disagreeable it is to attempt to figure out which message is to be disregarded and which taken seriously. To illustrate: Was the "stone face" that greeted you with a "Good morning!" at the door of the church, after the service of worship this past Sunday, meant to intimidate you? Was it saying, "Well, here's one parishioner who never will have much good to say about you, now that you've preached *that* sermon"? Or was it saying simply, "I'd like to wish you the best of good mornings, but I had a tooth pulled yesterday and frankly, my jaw still aches; so I hope the words will sound right, despite how I look"? Or was the "stone face" saying nothing at all of any consequence? Was it there merely by habit, and not by intent? As Eisenberg and Smith have asserted, it often is not especially easy to interpret accurately the significance or insignificance of kinesic behavior—"the visual aspects of non-verbal . . . communication."[3] That being the case, it would seem wise for preachers to do everything in their power to make sure that their body language reinforces their words and their so-called paralanguage of vocal tone, rate, pitch, and volume.[4]

Preachers *can* learn to control their bodies. It may not always be easy or comfortable, but it certainly is possible. In fact, research in kinesics over the last several years apparently has yielded evidence to indicate that all people learn to use facial expression, posture, movement, and gestures of the arms and hands consciously, to conceal or to reveal their feelings, to affect others, to win acceptance, or even to generate hostility or to promote disquiet or discomfort. We play numerous roles in a variety of contexts, and in order to protect ourselves from unprincipled manipulation and to draw forth from other people the kinds of responses that may be regarded as in some sense gratifying to us, we control our bodies; we make them obey our minds, our hearts, our wills.[5] Have you not ever held back tears, or perhaps a smile—which is harder to do, by the way—just because the time and the place did not seem right to weep or to let that two-dimpled grin spread happily across your face? And have you not thought twice about raising your hand in a classroom, or about frowning in discontent in the face of someone who said something that sounded quite incomprehensible to you? Kinesic behavior, even in the most informal kinds of circumstances, and in purely interpersonal, one-to-one relationships, is at least partially rule-governed and deliberate. We do not indulge impulse at all times. Quite the contrary, we often choose postures, looks, and the movements of our extremities as carefully as we choose our words. In fact, our choices are to some extent predictable, for people's kinesic repertoires are as limited as their vocabularies.[6] We are not free to let our bodies do with us as they will; and we are not free simply to do with them as we please. Always there are constraints; and so it is with preaching.

In preaching, we are not merely emoting—we are endeavoring to kindle people's imaginations, to persuade them to think with us, feel with us, react with us, to some probing of human experience by the Word of God. As I have indicated previously, we are speaking in order to facilitate other people's listening. Our kinesic behavior, therefore, should not draw attention to itself and so become the object of our listeners' scorn or praise, fascination or disinterest, pleasure or discomfort. It should not communicate our frazzled determination to "get into" our sermons, or make obvious our need to find release from possible tensions. If we have a case of nerves, we simply will have to settle ourselves by concentrating upon what we are about. Pacing, bouncing, rocking, and wildly gesturing—or wiping a fevered brow that in reality is not fevered at all—may help us feel better and more relaxed; but such miscellaneous activity does not make us *look* relaxed, and certainly it does nothing to aid those who, it is hoped, are making some attempt to understand what we have to say. Rather, all that we do, from toe tip to hairline, ought to appear natural, and thus unobtrusive and suitable for promoting our own and our congregations' listening. Of the art of painting, Andrew Wyeth is alleged to have remarked:

> My aim is to escape from the medium with which I work; to leave no residue of technical mannerisms to stand between my expression and the observer . . . not to exhibit craft, but rather to submerge it and make it rightfully the hand-maiden of beauty, power, and emotional content. [7]

Of course, none of us preachers will manage literally to escape from our medium, for in the case of preaching, the medium is the self. [8] Still, Wyeth's concern for technical control, so that mannerisms can be avoided, and so that one's craft can be properly submerged and made the handmaiden of the experience one is intending to evoke, is apropos of our task. The elementals of kinesic behavior appropriate to the preaching moment, consequently, need to be learned and put into practice.

One of the elementals of kinesic behavior appropriate to the preaching moment has to do with posture and gross body movements, the shifting and distribution of weight, trunk movements and shoulder positions—tipped forward, pulled backward, slouched, or squarely upright. For years people concerned with the aesthetics of body movement have maintained that posture and gross movements effectively suggest the intensity of speakers' basic moods and attitudes toward their subject matter and toward those with whom their subject matter is being shared. Recent empirical research, furthermore, has tended to corroborate what intuitively has been surmised. [9] Grabbing your pulpit, knuckles white, arms braced, weight stiffly distributed evenly on both feet, shoulders thrust back, *does* say something about you in relation to what you are trying to communicate and also to those with whom you are communicating. Maybe it says that you are ready to attack your listeners and your thoughts with fierce determination! Maybe it says that you are nearly scared to death of both! Maybe it says that you are filled with anxiety about the possibility of losing your thoughts and your listeners' attention! Whatever the specific emotion, you are feeling it up to the hilt; your muscles are tensed; your torso is bone stiff, committed to some terrible affect! But if your shoulders are slumped forward, your head dumped down toward your notes, and half your weight is slung upon your arms, both resting heavily on your pulpit, that posture also has something to say. It says that you are relaxed—limp—perhaps even to the point of indifference. Apparently neither your thoughts and feelings nor your attitude toward your listeners, is making much difference to you. You seem mentally and physically "tuned out" of what you are doing. Your body is sighing a "ho-hum" as audible, figuratively speaking, as any to which you might give voice.

These two examples of body posture and movement—or immobility!—obviously are exaggerated stereotypes. Still, they do raise the issue of controlling the kinesic behaviors when preaching, so that what is being said nonverbally and visually is suited both to the preaching situation and to the thought that is being communicated through the preacher's use of voice and language. The answer, I think, lies in a realization of how large gestures of the arms and hands, shoulder movements, and shifts and distributions of weight are related to what I shall call the preacher's "center."[10] The center is approximately the midpoint of the upper torso. Specifically, it may be designated as the area just below the sternum or breast bone. It is to this center that body movements and gestures are related. If the center moves in the direction of a specific gesture, that gesture usually is perceived as having some strength. If the "center" does not move in the direction of the gesture, on the other hand, the gesture appears rather weak and halfhearted, since the body seemingly has not been committed to what the arms and hands may be doing. To experiment, wave a greeting with your right hand to imaginary friends you see at some distance to your right. They are approaching you. Keep your center at right angles to your friends' approach, however. In other words, turn only your head to the right to recognize their presence. Once you have thus begun your greeting, turn your center toward them, and instead of keeping your weight evenly distributed, shift your feet in the direction of your friends, your right foot taking the lead and most of your weight. The waving gesture now seems stronger, more fully meant, doesn't it? The reason: You have just put your body and your weight where your attention has been directed. You have committed yourself fully to the gesture of greeting and welcome.

Similarly, in preaching, if your center leans in the direction of your listeners, it suggests assertiveness on your part, a measure of commitment to what you are saying, and it makes your listeners the focus of your attention and concern. If the center retracts, it signals some reserve and perhaps a withdrawal of attention from your listeners, in favor of the thought you want them to consider with you. If the center is held in pause—if it is moved neither assertively nor reflectively—its "at rest" position conceivably could indicate a patient holding and internalizing of thought, a personalizing and evaluating of ideas. Then again, if the center rocks from side to side, one might infer that indecision is the mood of the moment—that perhaps you are not quite sure how to relate to your thoughts or to your listeners. The rocking movement, on occasion, may be one of conscious choice. More often than not, however, it is accidental and inappropriate.

To avoid that nervous rocking of the center, position your feet comfortably far apart, one slightly in front of the other, and lean your weight into the balls of your feet. Now, in order to rock from port to starboard or vice versa without falling over, you will have to alter the position of your feet and the distribution of your weight consciously. The foot position just described, I think, is the best one to assume when you enter the pulpit. It takes no great concentration, and the position will leave you free to respond meaningfully to what you are saying, to your purpose in saying it, and to the congregation gathered before you.

Another of the elementals of kinesic behavior appropriate to the preaching moment has to do with facial expression. The gross body movements may indicate basic attitudes and degrees of intensity in affective response in preaching, but it is the face that communicates specific emotions and what kinesic scientists have called "affect blends."[11] Research has indicated, for example, that even across cultural and situational lines, certain primary emotional states— happiness, anger, fear, surprise, sadness, disgust/contempt, and interest—can be "read" accurately by individuals watching and listening to other people.[12] Beyond such primary emotions, however, innumerable complexities of response to situations, thoughts, and persons, can be expressed by the human face—more, in fact, than can be noted, understood, interpreted, and profitably used.[13] It is just as possible to overwhelm people with facial activity, in other words, as to distract them with incessant gesturing and excessive body movement, or with vocal mannerisms and articulatory faults. Preachers are not in pulpits for the purpose of putting their faces on display. They are not there to confess with their faces every nuance of affective response of which they are capable. They are there to preach, to embody and to "body-forth" some authentic reaction to a perceived Word of God. As body movements and gestures are meant not to draw attention to themselves, but to enable others to hear and to respond to the thought that is commanding the attention of the preacher, so facial expressions also need to be appropriate to what is being said, and they need to be suited to the preacher's homiletical intent.

However, the overdoing of facial expression is not a problem for very many preachers today; reticence in expression is the more common malady. Facial unresponsiveness, or what I call the neutral mask—which, of course, is also a type of expression—is pervasive. Perhaps it is indicative of people's desire not to open themselves and their feelings too readily to the possibility of acceptance or rejection—it may be self-protective. Or perhaps the neutral mask is indicative of the mood of our times—times that seem to favor staying "cool," detached, and objective, as opposed to being subjectively involved. Both these explanations for the rather regular appearance of the neutral mask have been given, and both may contain germs of truth.

Whatever the reasons for reticence in facial expression, however, one thing is certain: The appearance of the phenomenon almost invariably is associated with sluggish or careless articulation, as a result of very restricted jaw movement in the shaping of vowel sounds and consonants. It has been noted that some thirty-one muscles may be required to alter facial expression. If that is so, it would seem that any muscular activity in the face, particularly in the cheeks and jaw, would be advantageous in developing facial responsiveness to people, to thoughts, and to the experiences that preachers intend to evoke in their sermons.

If you suspect, or if your homiletics instructor or fellow students or colleagues tell you that you are inclined to put on the neutral mask, try this exercise. Speak a sentence, such as the opening line of the Prologue in Shakespeare's *King Henry* V, with all the gusto and exaggerated mouthing of the words that you can manage. Shove into your mouth an imaginary apple, if you must, and practice around it, over it, beneath it, behind it, in front of it, and despite it, "O for a muse of fire that would ascend the brightest heaven of invention!" If the facial activity becomes too extreme, one of your associates can tell you, and you can cut back easily enough. The hard task of the reticent speaker, after all, is not to intuit when too much is too much, but to be aware when too little is not enough. If your habit is reticence, go ahead and exaggerate, and leave it to others to tell you how much and what kind of cutting back, if any, may be necessary. Certainly it is worth the risk of one moment's extravagance, to free your face from the neutral mask, so that it can indicate your thoughts and feelings more completely as you preach.

The most important function of facial expression in preaching, however, is to enable preachers to indicate as fully and as appropriately as possible the full range of their responses to the experiences evoked in their sermons, so that their listeners can react empathically to what they say. It is common knowledge that people, at least to some extent, will react to authentic expressions of apprehension with apprehension, to delight with delight, to austere consideration of a thought with austerity, and to expressions of conviction and determination with a measure of willingness to be persuaded.[14] Actors, of course, rely upon audience empathy to help them make believable the perhaps realistic, but not actual, worlds they inhabit on the stage. Preachers, on the other hand, in the actuality of the preaching event, depend upon listener response to give that event a portion of the reality it is meant to have. Preaching is not only the preacher's task; it is also the task of those who gather to hear—and to see—what the preacher has to say. It is not only the preacher's thoughts, convictions, and attitudes concerning specific experiences of contemporary life that are challenged and redirected by the Word of God—it happens among the preacher's listeners, also; and that happening is what preaching really is about. Words signify what in truth is going on in the persons of those who preach and of those who listen. Consequently, if nothing is happening in those persons—if there is no apparent physical, reflective, and affective change, great or small, occurring in them—then the words being spoken, for all intents and purposes, signify nothing at all; then the sermon is actual, but not real. That your sermons may be real, give body to your thoughts—and thought to your body—and let what is on your mind and heart find appropriate expression on your face. If you need help and some guided experiences, I recommend that you return to the third chapter, "Preaching and the Imaginations of the Heart." Work through the exercises aloud once more and, as you do so, concentrate upon giving physical response—particularly facial response—to everything you are asked to picture, or hear, or smell, or taste.

The last of the elementals of kinesic behavior appropriate to the preaching moment that will be discussed concerns eye contact, and as Clyde Fant has indicated, the principal point of contact for preachers is the gathered congregation.[15] Preaching, after all, is conversational in character, as we have pointed out. It is direct. It is person to person; and those persons sitting in pews on Sunday morning, or gathered elsewhere at other times to attend to what you have to say, must be considered. Their nonverbal feedback needs to be "read," taken to heart, allowed to have impact upon your sermons as they are being delivered. It may be that you won't change a word of your prepared text. It may be that the arrangement of your ideas, anecdotes, and images will remain the same, as you survey the reactions of your listeners. Still, those listeners, if you truly look at them, will affect you. Their attention will quicken your concentration. Their apparent agreement will kindle your conviction. Their seeming bafflement will slow you down and may cause you to speak in a more reflective and less assertive manner. You cannot share a happy story with a friend, without that friend's smile or laugh or sheer interest heightening your own enjoyment, both of the story itself and of the telling. So, in preaching, you cannot look at your listeners and "read" their responses to you, to what you are saying, and how you are saying it, without in some way being moved. The preaching moment is as much your listeners' moment as your own. Therefore, establish direct contact with those listeners—see faces—note postures—catch eyes! Do not think for an instant that people are interested merely in observing *you*, for they are not. Rather they are interested in sharing with you in the proclamation of the gospel. They want and expect to be led in a creative hearing of the Word of God; and they want and expect to be encouraged in their response to it.

Direct eye contact with listeners, however, is not the only sort of eye contact that is possible and desirable in preaching. There is also indirect eye contact. Your eyes may focus for an instant or two upon a thought, as if, for example, sitting in a lecture hall, you took the focus of your attention away from the lecturer and placed it upon something he or she said—some idea that troubled or fascinated you and that set you to mulling just a bit. Your eyes may suggest that, with your imagination, you see something happening in front of you and in front of your listeners, in the very moment of proclamation. Your eyes may trace an imaginary movement of objects or persons. They may position a character who is being described—the central character of an illustrative story or anecdote, or a scriptural or literary allusion. In that case, you will find that your eyes actually will fasten on a spot somewhere between the center and right or left edge of your congregation, over the heads of the people gathered before you. Then again, your eyes may indicate your listening for sounds. They may dart back and forth momentarily till they settle on the imaginary sound source. In conversation and storytelling, we do that kind of thing all the time, don't we?—especially in storytelling to children, when we are attempting to make the story come alive. "Listen! 'The rattle of gunfire is close at hand,' " the storyteller said.[16] Did you hear it? No? Then listen again. Listen, as it were, with your eyes.

Remember this, too: Indirect eye contact can be focused upon one's self. Your attention can move inward. You can give consideration to your feelings, your most private thoughts, and seemingly, for a brief period, you can avoid contact with anything "out there." In point of fact, your glance actually will be downward and away from your listeners; but you will not fasten on anything external to yourself. You will not take note of things—sight or sound images, smells, or tastes—and you will not react directly to them. Instead, the drift of your attention will be away from objective realities, whether fictive or actual, and toward the subjective reality with which you are attempting to come to grips. Your mood, therefore, will be one of introspection.

To more completely understand my meaning, repeat the following words from the first stanza of a famous poem by W. H. Auden and, throughout the first five lines, avoid any contact with people, either actual or imaginary. In other words, do not look up from the text—at least not very far up. Yet, do not concentrate long upon the words themselves: See them; get them in mind; but then let them go out of focus. Focus your attention instead upon Auden's mood of grief and loss: He is recalling the death of a poet friend. Let the grief and loss become your own; dwell on the frozen, shapeless pain until you can barely stand it. Then, at the very end of the stanza, as you speak the last line, look up and engage your listeners directly, in quiet, taut conversation. "Eyeball to eyeball," let them share your grief. You are bridging the gap between subjectivity and objectivity. In commenting upon the experience of grief into which you have just entered, you are beginning to distance yourself and your listeners from it.

> He disappeared in the dead of winter:
> The brooks were frozen, the airports almost deserted,
> And snow disfigured the public statues;
> The mercury sank in the mouth of the dying day.
> O all the instruments agree
> The day of his death was a dark cold day.[17]

We have now completed our consideration of the elementals of kinesic behavior appropriate to the preaching moment. The intention has not been to make anyone self-conscious. Rather, we have attempted to develop consciousness of the body talk we all normally engage in and to adapt that body talk to the specific formal constraints of the preaching situation. These constraints operate upon us all, but how we respond to them in specific instances of proclamation is a very unique and personal thing for each of us. Ultimately, no one can tell us exactly how we ought to stand, move, gesture, and look, in the pulpit. But we all can help one another to see how we ought *not* to look or stand or move; and we can appraise one another's homiletical efforts in light of the facts and understandings of kinesic behavior we have discussed. We can evaluate *ourselves*, also, with the use of video tape. As was the case with voice usage, however, self-evaluation always needs to be checked against evaluations received from others, for when we attend to our own preaching, our inclination is to hear what we expect and want to hear and to see what we expect and want to see. Trust yourself, of course; but look to your fellow students and instructors and colleagues and lay listeners for help, as well. If you do, I think you will not regret it.

VIII. THE PREACHING MOMENT
REVISITED

There is, of course, a sense in which the preaching moment never can be revisited. Like all moments, when it is past, it is past; and there can be no going back to it. The preaching moment cannot be frozen in ink; it cannot be recorded on tape. Sermons can be both written and recorded, obviously; but anyone who has read or heard a sermon after the moment of its preaching knows how much of the preaching moment itself is missing and how little of the event of that moment is kept or recalled. Clyde Fant, among others, even has worked out an approach to the composition of sermons, based upon the unique quality of the preaching moment as an irreducible oral/aural event.[1] His conviction, rightly held, I think, is that preaching cannot be thought of simply as the delivery of a manuscript. Rather, in the words of Dwight Stevenson and Charles Diehl, preaching must be thought of as a moment of "intense integration."[2] Not only before the preaching moment, but in it, listening and composing—or at least recomposing—are engaged in, along with thinking and feeling and speaking. And the work of preaching is not accomplished only by the person who speaks. Those who listen also have their role to play. They listen and compose—that is, make of the sermon what they can or will—think and feel and give expression to their thoughts and feelings. Listeners, in other words, provide those who preach, and also provide one another with "feedback." The true significance of the preaching moment, therefore, is in the moment itself, and cannot be extracted from it.[3] What it is, it is but once, and once only.

Yet, in at least two ways, preaching moments can be revisited. They can be revisited as an old haunt is revisited, not to capture again what was, but to see what the experience of the place may hold for people now. A sermon can be repeated, can be preached more than once, can be recorded and later played back, can be written down and read at some other time. The original preaching moment, in all its uniqueness, is not thus brought back to life, but the sermon still can have significance. The situation when people hear it or read it may be different; the people, having heard the sermon before, may be different, and therefore bring something to it and take something from it that could not have been brought or taken before. Still, continuity is there. The words are there; the manner of their expression may be there. The old haunt no longer is what it used to be, but it is the old haunt, and nobody can say that it is not.

More to our immediate purpose, however, preaching moments can be revisited for the sake of criticism. The record of them written and recorded on audio or video tape can be consulted, and aspects of sermons can be judged in the light of appropriate criteria.[4] All serious-minded folk thus revisit their moments of accomplishment and evaluate them. If they do not, their labors sooner or later become undisciplined, their work shoddy. When it comes to any kind of skilled effort—and preaching requires skilled effort—there can be no acceptance of the status quo; there can be no mere maintenance of one's level of performance; there can be no satisfaction with what euphemistically is labeled "good enough." There can be only change: growth in ability, or gradual disability; new insights into our tasks as preachers are provoked, or insight falters altogether. Our skills are honed, or they are lost; our habits of thought are modified, or we end up at the mercy of "the ideas that use us."[5] Bricklayers, plumbers, doctors, lawyers, all, criticize their own work—not to denigrate it, but to improve it; and artists do the same, and so do preachers. Preachers do not "nitpick," fuss over trivia, and simply belittle themselves and one another. That goes without saying; serious criticism, after all, is not mere fault-finding. Yet if they care at all about what they are called to do, preachers do weigh in the balance the fruits of their labors, and when some lack is discerned, at least an attempt is made to correct the situation. The problem in criticism, then, is to develop appropriate criteria by which sermons can be evaluated, lacks discerned, and corrective steps taken.

When it comes to sermon *delivery*, such criteria already are at hand in the *principles* of sermon delivery earlier presented and discussed. The first of those principles, you will recall, indicated that you should attend to the movement of thought in preaching and be prepared to move with it, for preaching that is true preaching never will let you rest content with some static arrangement of ideas. Further, it was stated that movement of thought in preaching implies conflict: conflicting ideas, attitudes, convictions; conflicts within and between people; conflicts between people and things, between forces in nature and civilized life; conflicts between life itself and death; conflicts subtle and not so subtle; conflicts that include us and that we sometimes cause. Preaching that is alive is preaching that in some sense directly expresses or implies conflict; and in the development of that conflict, there is a point of turning (the fulcrum of the text, as we called it), a climax, and a denouement. In evaluating your sermon delivery in terms of movement of thought, therefore, it would seem appropriate to ask yourself these questions: (1) What is the principal conflict expressed or implied in the sermon? (2) How is the conflict developed? (3) Where is the point of turning—the fulcrum—in the manner of development of conflict? (4) Where is the climax? (5) Where is the denouement or resolution of the conflict? (6) Can the conflict, fulcrum, climax, and denouement of the text be heard and felt as the sermon is preached? In answering, be sure to rely primarily upon some record of the sermon *as delivered*—video or audio tape recording, and the critical comments of listeners. Do not rely primarily upon a previously composed manuscript, notes, outline, or brief, for such materials constitute preparation for the preaching moment. What you are after now is evaluation of that moment itself.

The second principle of sermon delivery which may be used as a criterion for evaluation, stipulates that preachers should attend to the specific contexts that give rise to the movement of thought in their sermons and be aware of their personal involvement with those contexts, for in preaching, ideas never are abstract. They are grounded in past, present, and emerging situations of human life. Preachers, in other words, need to speak empathically, with color, and with sensitivity to compositional context. They need to respond to the imagistic appeals of statements made in their sermons—the sight, sound, olfactory, gustatory, tactile, visceral, and kinesthetic images described earlier. They need to express themselves in such a way that their responses to those imagistic appeals are evidenced. In addition, preachers need to stay alert to the conceptual relationship of specific images. Images, in other words, are not to be indulged in for their own sake, but are to be used in order to accomplish something—to make a point. To evaluate your expression of involvement with the experiential contexts that give rise to the movement of thought in your sermon, then, you might ask: (1) What types of imagistic appeals are present in the sermon? (2) How are the imagistic appeals of the sermon related conceptually? (3) Does the delivery of the sermon evidence some sort of response to the imagistic appeals present in it? (4) Do expressed responses to imagistic appeals seem appropriate, in light of the compositional context? Obviously the last question in particular requires some exercise of judgment on the part of all those involved in evaluation of the preaching moment. Opinions may differ with regard to whether or not expressed responses to imagistic appeals seem appropriate. The relative merits of conflicting opinions, however, should be judged on the basis of how comprehensively they take into account relevant details of imagery, word color, and conceptualization; and because preachers usually will tend to hear and see in their preaching efforts what they expect or want to hear and see, it is recommended that they trust the informed judgments of others more than their own. If preachers, in fact, subject their opinions in all matters to the possibility of corroboration or contradiction by others who have insight into homiletical criticism, their appraisals of their work no doubt may be more confidently employed in developing a thorough understanding of the requirements of responsible homiletical practice and in sharpening preaching skills.

The third principle of sermon delivery used here as an evaluative criterion has to do with responding to the claim made upon preachers and listeners alike in the course of proclamation of the gospel and the consequent establishment of overall mood in the preaching moment: Allow yourself to hear the claim made upon you when you preach. For preaching, after all, makes use of religious/metaphoric language, which has the power to disclose new ways—perhaps challenging, or even uncomfortable, but responsible ways—of being and acting in the world. The contention is that, in and through any and all other forms of conflict that give movement to thought in preaching, there is a current of conflict between the human and the divine wills. There is the tragedy of our desire to be gods unto ourselves, despite our need of God and our need to trust in him. There is the comedic fact that, despite that tragic pause in which we stand, God has spoken and acted to make us his own in Christ. Further, in doing that, he has disclosed life as he intends it to be, rather than as we intend it for ourselves. In Christ, that is to say, God takes human word-created worlds and transforms them into realities that are good or pleasing to him. God exercises his lordship over us, despite us, and he wills and acts to have us as his own. Further, the claim thus made upon us in preaching can have specific or nonspecific implications. In other words, what, in any particular circumstance of life, we ought to do about the fact that God in Christ owns us individually and corporately, along with everything we have and are, may be spelled out or may be left indefinite. In either case, however, some sort of reaction is called for from the preacher. That reaction may range all the way from joyful, ready acceptance and celebration of God's claim upon human life, to an almost anguished or apprehensive affirmation of it. Whatever the preacher's reaction, when established, it will give a sense of purpose and basic mood to the preaching moment. The moment will have a definite ambience, and something significant—life or death, a gain or a loss, meaning or nothingness—will appear to be at stake. To evaluate effectiveness in sermon delivery in terms of the criterion just discussed, it would seem appropriate to raise the questions: (1) How was the claim of God upon human life registered in and through the sermon? (2) Were the implications of the claim spelled out or left indefinite? (3) What kind of reaction to the claim of God upon human life was expressed in the preaching moment? (4) Was the reaction to that claim expressed with enough intensity to give the sermon a sense of purpose and to indicate that, in the proclamation of the gospel, something significant was at stake?

The fourth and last principle of sermon delivery which may be used as a criterion in evaluation of preaching, asserts that preachers, along with their listeners, are to "give ear to" the explicit or implicit kerygma that lends coherence to their sermons and that sustains them in their efforts to relate the world of religious experience evoked in scripture to the experience of people today. Preaching, that is to say, involves a personalizing of the gospel, a presentation of a Christian interpretation of life, in some way unique to the person doing the interpreting, and preachers and their listeners should be aware of that personalization of the gospel. The questions concerning contemporary situations that preachers see raised in the Scriptures, for example, are the questions *they* see; other people might not see those questions as being raised at all. The elements of the New Testament kerygma, which particular preachers feel need to be especially emphasized at a given moment, likewise are elements *they* feel need emphasis; other people might very well choose differently. And those conditions of personal and corporate existence in the modern world, which certain preachers may think need an immediate critique, are the conditions that trouble *them*; some individuals, on the other hand, may consider other matters more pressing. Of course, responsible preachers will remain open to criticism of their choices and to modification of their interpretative stance in the light of scholarship—past and present—and the development and presentation of alternative hermeneutical method-ologies. Still, personalization of the gospel will occur when they preach. Choices will be made by them, and as a result, the gospel will become *their* gospel, and the Christ, whose gospel they make their own in the course of its proclamation, will become *their* Christ. Preachers, consequently, also will stay aware of the fact that what they say in their sermons is not the whole truth, but only a partial and necessarily tentative witness to the truth. Other people's considera-tion of what the gospel means, therefore, will be respected; and preachers will speak in such a way as to evidence their respect of others' opinions. Their speaking style will be conversational, not declamatory. They will, as it were, stand *with* their listeners, not above them, as if somehow they were in possession of truths to be dispensed. And further, they will observe and encourage their listeners' right to critical involvement in the preaching moment. Their listeners' attention, naturally enough, will be sought and it is hoped, held, but any attempt to manipulate the listeners' response will be eschewed; the listeners' right to respond on the basis of their own insight and sense of the truth will be respected. In evaluating a preaching effort in light of this fourth principle of sermon delivery, therefore, I would recommend that the following questions be raised: (1) In this preaching moment, how were the Scriptures used to delineate and to address current issues in individual and corporate life? (2) What kerygmatic elements came into play in the interpretative process? (3) What, if anything, was done to invite listeners' critical consideration of the Christian interpretation of life proffered in the sermon? For example, was there use of appropriate direct eye contact with listeners, a conversational inflectional pattern, an attitude of listening with, as opposed to talking at, those attending to what was being said? (4) Were listeners apparently left free to respond on the basis of their own insight and sense of truth, or was there some evidence of an attempt to direct and to prescribe response?

A further consideration in evaluation of preachers' efforts in the preaching moment has to do with matters of voice and articulation; and as indicated in the preceding chapter, the concern here is not with vocal technique and precision in articulation for their own sakes, but with the development of vocal responsiveness and clarity in expression of thought. Listening preachers, after all, are not expected simply to be listening to themselves; and those who attend to what preachers have to say certainly should not be subjected to the unhappy task of having to listen to preachers listening to themselves! On the contrary, preachers and listeners alike are expected to be attending to the movement of thought in sermons; to the experiential contexts that give rise to any movement of thought; to the claim upon people's individual and corporate life registered in sermons; and to the kerygmatic elements present which give those sermons coherence and uniqueness, as an attempt is made in and through them to gain insight into the relevance of the gospel for the conduct of contemporary affairs, in the light of scriptural witness to God's saving activity in the world in Jesus Christ. Still, in preaching, it is possible to be conscious of self without being self-conscious. And in homiletical criticism, it is possible to give some consideration to the subject of voice and articulation without being distracted from matters of primary concern. In fact, it is precisely when something about preachers' habits of voice or articulation causes distraction, that need for work in this area is most in evidence. Breath support of the voice in preaching, for example, should be adequate for proper development of a line of thought. It should be related to phrasing; and conversely, one's development of a line of thought should not be at the mercy of breathing habits that necessitate pausing for gulps of air at those very moments when sense dictates that speaking ought to continue. Similarly, in phonation—initiation of voice—freedom from tightness, breathiness, and glottal attack is vital in order that the voice may be heard, may be capable of expression of a wide range of thoughts and moods, and that it may not call attention to itself because of persistent darkness or brightness of tone, or hypo- or hypernasality. Finally, clarity in articulation is essential in order that what is being heard and felt and thought by preachers may be fully understood by their listeners. The goal is not "prissiness" or "pronounciness"—the terms most often used to describe self-conscious and overly precise articulation. The goal is communication! In evaluating voice and articulation in sermon delivery, then, it would seem appropriate to ask: (1) Was breath support adequate for sensible phrasing and meaningful variation in rate, in the development of thought? (2) Was the voice produced with freedom, and was it capable of response to the various qualitative demands of ideas and images present in the sermons? (3) Was there sufficient and balanced resonation of the voice so that it could be heard easily and yet not draw attention to itself? (4) Was there clarity in articulation so that what was being said could be fully understood?

The last consideration in evaluation of the preaching moment has to do with the listening preacher's body talk; and body talk, just as was the case with voice and articulation, is not meant to draw attention to itself. Instead, posture, movement and gestures of the arms and hands, facial expression, and eye contact should give support to what the preacher is saying and should be suited to the preacher's purpose in saying it. In other words, language, paralanguage—that is, voice quality, rate, pitch, and volume—and kinesic behavior (the visual aspects of nonverbal communication) should all be saying the same thing. When there is conflict among them, some confusion in the perception of meaning by listeners is almost inevitable. Gross body movements and gestures may be either strong or weak, as determined by their relationship to the preacher's center. They may be tense or almost flaccid, but they should not seem inadvertent and irrelevant. Rather, they should seem nearly inevitable in light of what the preacher is trying to communicate. Similarly, facial expression may range all the way from apparent indifference to joy or deep sadness. Yet it should not be exaggerated or overdone; and whether it is indicative of strong feeling or carefully avoids any strong feeling, it should not be merely habitual. On the contrary, the preacher's face ought to give specific expression to what is on the mind and heart as a result of imaginative involvement with the experience a sermon is intended to evoke.

Then, too, there is the matter of eye contact. The principal point of contact, of course, is the congregation, for the preacher will want to see and to take account of the listeners' responses. As has been indicated several times throughout this text, listeners are not mere spectators at a preaching event—they are fully a part of it. They have their own contribution to make in the proclamation of the gospel. Still, there will be occasions when indirect eye contact is called for; preachers will want to focus concentration on sight or sound images or on intrapersonal moods. Again, the important thing to bear in mind is the appropriateness of the eye contact, in light of the preacher's thought and his or her purpose in sharing that thought. Remember, where the preacher's eyes focus—that is where the congregation's attention is directed. To determine whether or not a preacher's body talk—gross body movements and gestures, facial expressions, and eye contact—is effective and appropriate in terms of the peculiar constraints of the preaching situation, the following questions could be asked during evaluation of the sermon: (1) Were the preacher's posture, body movements, and gestures apparently suited to what was being said and to the preacher's purpose in saying it? (2) Were movements and gestures, whether strong or weak, intense or relaxed, sufficiently motivated; and were they appropriately related to the preacher's center? (3) Were facial expressions seemingly indicative of specific feelings derived from the preacher's involvement with the experiences evoked in the sermon? (4) Was there sufficient direct eye contact with listeners? And was such indirect eye contact as was established during the course of delivery of the sermon effective in directing attention to sight or sound images, or to intrapersonal moods?

So the preaching moment now has been revisited for purposes of criticism of sermon delivery. There always will be such moments of visitation and critique, for no preacher ever has "arrived." All of them—all of *us*—continually are *en route*. And that, I think, is about as hopeful a thought as any with which I could end this booklong consideration of the preaching moment. Think of it: Not what we are, are we; but what we are to become—*that* is what we are!

NOTES

A WORD TO THE READER

1. W. H. Auden, "In Memory of W. B. Yeats," *Selected Poetry of W. H. Auden* (New York: Random House, 1958), p. 53.

CHAPTER I—THE TALK NEVER IS ALL

1. Robert Frost, "Home Burial," *The Poetry of Robert Frost*, ed. by Edward Connery Lathem (New York: Holt, Rhinehart & Winston, 1969), pp. 54-55.
2. Harold A. Brack, "The Listening Preacher," *Religious Communication Today* (September 1978), pp. 18-19.
3. For a discussion of the uniqueness of personal perception with implications for theological reflection, see C. Daniel Batson, J. Christian Beker, and W. Malcolm Clark, *Commitment Without Ideology: The Experience of Christian Growth* (Philadelphia: United Church of Christ Press, 1973), especially pp. 45-47.
4. Martin Heidegger, *Poetry, Language, Thought*, trans. by Albert Hofstadter (New York: Harper & Row, 1971), pp. 20-57.
5. Shakespeare, *A Midsummer Night's Dream*, act 5, sc. 1.
6. Herbert H. Farmer, *The Servant of the Word* (Philadelphia: Fortress Press, 1964), pp. 66-88.
7. For an exploration of the disorienting and reorienting function of Jesus' parables, see Norman Perrin, *Jesus and the Language of the Kingdom: Symbol and Metaphor in New Testament Interpretation* (Philadelphia: Fortress Press, 1976), especially p. 125.
8. John Macquarrie, *God Talk: An Examination of the Language and Logic of Theology* (New York: Harper & Row, 1967). A succinct and compelling discussion of the literal, referential use of language as contrasted with various other kinds of language functions, particularly the religious use of language, can be found in Frederick Ferre, *Language, Logic and God* (New York: Harper & Brothers, 1961).

9. TeSelle, Sallie McFague, *Speaking in Parables: A Study in Metaphor and Theology* (Philadelphia: Fortress Press, 1975).

10. Charles H. Dodd, *The Apostolic Preaching and Its Developments* (London: Hodder and Stoughton, 1936), p. 96.

11. Farmer, *Servant of the Word*, pp. 44-49.

12. The concept of the referent for a text of scripture (and consequently for a sermonic text based upon scripture) lying "in front of" rather than "behind" the text is explicated in David Tracy, *Blessed Rage for Order: The New Pluralism in Theology* (New York: Seabury Press, 1975), pp. 77-78.

13. This "two-world walk" of the preacher, one foot in the world of the Bible and the history of theological reflection and the other in the contemporary scene, is discussed in Joseph Sittler, *The Ecology of Faith: The New Situation in Preaching* (Philadelphia: Muhlenberg Press, 1961).

CHAPTER II—THE SOUND OF SENSE IN PREACHING

1. A classic statement from the old expressionist school of speech of the ways in which reflective (ideas), affective (attitudes), and effective (convictions) qualities of thought can find expression, sometimes with one or another of the qualities dominant, sometimes with all the qualities thoroughly mixed and at full force, can be found in Leland Powers and Carol Hoyt Powers, *Fundamentals of Expression* (Boston: T. Groom & Co., 1916), pp. 21-27, 35-38. Powers speaks of "mental," "moral," and "vital" qualities. And homileticians have spoken of preaching to "the whole man"—not just to a person's head. It matters little what words are used to indicate what is meant here, I think. The point is this: Thoughts are complex occurrences of the mind, and their appropriate expression therefore requires that speakers be responsive to that fact.

2. Charlotte I. Lee, *Oral Interpretation* (New York: Houghton Mifflin Co., 1971), pp. 27-28. Also see Charlotte I. Lee, *Oral Reading of the Scripture* (New York: Houghton Mifflin Co., 1974), p. 146. Professor Lee uses the word "crisis" instead of "fulcrum" when referring to the turning point in prose. However, chiefly because of the motion (tipping and balancing) implied by the word, I have chosen to stay with "fulcrum" whether the turning point having to do with the development of conflict, and thus progression of thought, is in poetic or sermonic material.

3. A. R. Ammons, "Levitation," *Collected Poems 1951-1971* (New York: W. W. Norton & Co., 1972), p. 197.

4. For a brief, clear discussion of the concept of persona, see Lee, *Oral Interpretation*, pp. 23, 386, and *Oral Reading*, pp. 147-48. Also, for an example similar to the use in this book, see William Brower, "The Spiritual Benefits of Poetry," *Military Chaplain's Review* (Spring 1979), p. 54.

5. Frederick Buechner, "Anger," *Wishful Thinking* (New York: Harper & Row, 1973), p. 2.

CHAPTER III—PREACHING AND THE IMAGINATIONS OF THE HEART

1. Donald E. Phillips, "Karl Barth's Philosophy of Communication" (Ph.D. dissertation, The University of Oklahoma, 1977), p. 67.

2. John Bluck, *Beyond Neutrality: A Christian Critique of the Media* (Geneva, Switzerland: World Council of Churches, 1978), p. 25.
3. A strong case for the utter necessity of credibility in preaching is made by Marvin Dirks in "Credibility in Preaching," *Religious Communication Today*, (September 1978), pp. 20-22.
4. Walter J. Ong, *The Presence of the Word* (New Haven, Conn.: Yale University Press, 1967), pp. 117-22.
5. Harry Emerson Fosdick, "The Unknown Soldier," *Riverside Sermons* (New York: Harper & Brothers, 1958), p. 351.
6. All the exercises in word color were prepared by William Brower, Associate Director of Speech, Princeton Theological Seminary, Princeton, New Jersey, and are used with permission.
7. Edgar Allan Poe, "The Raven"; I Samuel 17:4; Thomas Hardy, "The Darkling Thrush"; Lord Byron, "She Walks in Beauty"; Daniel 5:1 (KJV).
8. Sara Lowrey and Gertrude E. Johnson, *Interpretative Reading* (New York: Appleton-Century-Crofts, 1953), pp. 30-62.
9. Frederick B. Speakman, "Converted at Every Revival," *Love Is Something You Do* (Westwood, N.J.: Fleming H. Revell, 1959), p. 109.
10. Walt Whitman, "Locusts," *Leaves of Grass*.
11. Shakespeare, *Macbeth*, act V, sc. 1.
12. Howard Nemerov, from "Santa Claus," *The Collected Poems of Howard Nemerov* (Chicago: University of Chicago Press, 1977), p. 238. By permission of the author.
13. Genesis 27:26-27.
14. Robert Penn Warren, from "The Patented Gate and the Mean Hamburger," *The Circus in the Attic and Other Stories* (New York: Harcourt, Brace, Jovanovich, 1947), pp. 125-26.
15. Edgar Allan Poe, "The Pit and the Pendulum."
16. Psalm 9:1-16.
17. Frost, "Birches," *The Poetry of Robert Frost*, ed. by Edward Connery Lathem (New York: Holt, Rhinehart & Winston, 1969), p. 122.
18. "A Musical Instrument," *The Poetical Works of Elizabeth Barrett Browning*, ed. Frederick G. Kenyon (New York: Macmillan, 1897). pp. 537-38.
19. Fosdick, "Forgiveness of Sins," *Riverside Sermons* (New York: Harper & Brothers, 1958), pp. 292-300.

CHAPTER IV—HEARING WHAT PREACHING EXPECTS OF US

1. Christina Rossetti, "The Thread of Life."
2. Shakespeare, *Macbeth*, act V, sc. 5.
3. Frost, "Mending Wall."
4. Helmut Thielicke, *Between God and Satan*, trans. by C. C. Barber (Grand Rapids, Mich.: Wm. B. Eerdmans Pub. Co., 1958), p. 4.
5. Frederick Buechner, *Telling the Truth: The Gospel as Tragedy, Comedy and Fairy Tale* (New York: Harper & Row, 1977), pp. 25-47.
6. Paul E. Scherer, "Let God Be God," *The Word God Sent* (Grand Rapids, Michigan: Baker Book House, 1977), p. 143. Original copyright (New York: Harper and Row, 1965).

7. Peter C. Hodgson, *Jesus—Word and Presence* (Philadelphia: Fortress Press, 1971), pp. 74-83.

8. Buechner, *Telling the Truth*, pp. 73-98.

9. Paul E. Scherer, in *Worship Resources for the Christian Year*, ed. by Charles L. Wallis (New York: Harper & Brothers, 1954), p. 333.

10. Buechner, *Telling the Truth*.

11. Lloyd F. Bitzer, "The Rhetorical Situation," *Philosophy and Rhetoric I*, (1968), pp. 1-14. For a helpful summary and positive critique of Bitzer's thought, see John H. Patton, "Causation and Creativity in Rhetorical Situations: Distinctions and Implications," *The Quarterly Journal of Speech*, no. 65 (1979), pp. 36-55.

12. Ernest T. Campbell, "The See-Saw View of Life," *The Princeton Seminary Bulletin* (March 1971), pp. 53-57. Used by permission.

13. George A. Buttrick, "The Name of the Nameless," *Sermons Preached in a University Church* (Nashville: Abingdon Press, 1959), pp. 164-71. Copyright © 1959 by Abingdon Press. Used by permission.

CHAPTER V—GOSPEL AND CONVERSATION IN PREACHING

1. The word of God is God's Word to us when it engages our thoughts in depth so that some form of vital response is elicited from us.

2. Farmer, *Servant of the Word*, pp. 89-109, especially p. 104.

3. Elizabeth Achtemeier, *The Old Testament and the Proclamation of the Gospel* (Philadelphia: Westminster Press, 1973), pp. 47-81, esp. 77-81.

4. Bruce M. Metzger, *The New Testament: Its Background, Growth and Content* (Nashville: Abingdon Press, 1965), p. 177.

5. A particularly apt example of how a preacher's "place of standing" relative to the gospel and contemporary life can change, is provided in Harry Emerson Fosdick, "The Church Must Go Beyond Modernism," *Riverside Sermons*, pp. 353-62.

6. A very interesting theory is offered by David S. Kaufer, "Point of View in Rhetorical Situations: Classical and Romantic Contrasts and Contemporary Implications," *The Quarterly Journal of Speech* (April 1979), pp. 171-86.

7. The question of authority in preaching is raised here, but since it is not specifically germane to the matter of sermon delivery, it is not discussed. I do want to mention, however, that my understanding of authority in preaching is that it is, first of all, derivative—issuing from the authenticity of response to the Word of God—and that it is also to be measured in terms of "yield" of homiletical insight into the implications of the gospel for contemporary life, as well as the preacher's openness to critical scrutiny of his or her ideas, responsibility in exegesis, and the traditional rhetorical factors that contribute to credibility.

8. As far as I am aware, Harry Emerson Fosdick was the first homiletician to proffer "animated conversation" as the most appropriate mode of sermon delivery. See Roy C. McCall, "Harry Emerson Fosdick: Paragon and Paradox," *The Quarterly Journal of Speech* (October 1952), p. 285.

9. Kaufer, "Point of View."

10. Sara Lowrey and Gertrude E. Johnson, *Interpretative Reading* (New York: Appleton-Century-Crofts, 1953), pp. 176-78.

11. Farmer, *Servant of the Word*, p. 49.

12. Richard Carl Hoefler, *Creative Preaching and Oral Writing* (Lima, Ohio: C. S. S. Publishing Co., 1978), p. 162.

13. For the description of effect of falling, rising, and circumflex inflections, I am indebted to W. J. Beeners, Professor of Speech, Princeton Theological Seminary.
14. Lowrey and Johnson, *Interpretative Reading*, pp. 168-76.
15.. Robert Frost, "Pertinax," *The Poetry of Robert Frost*, ed. by Edward Connery Lathem (New York: Holt, Rinehart & Winston, 1969), p. 308.

CHAPTER VI—VOICE AND ARTICULATION

1. For understanding the voice and articulation process in detail and for programs of study for voice improvement, I would recommend Jon Eisenson, *Voice and Diction* (New York: Macmillan & Co., 1974).
2. The vocal folds often are called cords. However, they actually resemble muscle tissue, having the appearance of lips. Therefore I have chosen to use the more descriptive term.
3. Voice and speech are functions overlaid on the vocal folds. The essential purpose of the folds is to keep foreign matter from entering the trachea.
4. Shakespeare.
5. There is lip rounding on the vowel sounds in such words as "boy," "boat," and "boot." However, such lip rounding plays no role in vowel shading as discussed here.
6. This vowel chart is a simplified adaptation of the much more scientifically rigorous and complete chart developed by Claude M. Wise, *Applied Phonetics*, © 1957, p. 96. Reprinted by permission of Prentice-Hall, Inc., Englewood Cliffs, New Jersey.
7. Shakespeare, *Hamlet*, act I, sc. 2.
8. Matthew 7:24-27.
9. Shakespeare, *King Henry V*, "Prologue."
10. Mark Van Doren, from "End," *Collected Poems* (New York: Hill & Wang, 1963). Copyright © 1963 by Mark Van Doren. Reprinted by permission of Hill & Wang (a division of Farrar, Straus & Giroux, Inc.).
11. Matthew Arnold, "Dover Beach."
12. Langston Hughes, "The Negro Speaks of Rivers," *Selected Poems of Langston Hughes* (New York: Alfred A. Knopf, 1959), p. 4. © 1926 by Alfred A. Knopf, Inc. and renewed 1954 by Langston Hughes.
13. Karl Shapiro, "Auto Wreck," *Collected Poems, 1940-1978* (New York: Random House, 1978), p. 6. © 1942 and renewed 1970 by Karl Shapiro.
14. Robert Frost, "After Apple-Picking," *The Poetry of Robert Frost*, ed. by Edward Connery Lathem (New York: Holt, Rinehart & Winston, 1969), p. 68.
15. Shakespeare, *Julius Caesar*, act III, sc. 2.
16. I Samuel 17:1, 4, 8-10.
17. Robert Herrick, "Upon a Child."
18. Psalm 46:10.

CHAPTER VII—THE LISTENING PREACHER'S BODY TALK

1. Conflicts between verbal, tonal, and kinesic messages sometimes may be tolerated in the speech of comedians. In humor, the very contradictions and conflicts may *be* the message.
2. In communications studies, there exists an entire field of investigation called

noise theory, having to do with the process of determining what is to be ignored in communication events. Noise is present in language usage, in the use of paralanguage, and in kinesic behavior. Noise elements at times even may be used purposively. For a brief definition, see Jerome Rothstein, "An Overview . . . From an Informational-Organizational-Operational Viewpoint," Lee Thayer, ed., *Communication: Concepts and Perspectives* (Washington, D.C.: Spartan Books, 1967), pp. 405-06.

3. Abne M. Eisenberg and Ralph R. Smith, Jr., *Nonverbal Communication* (New York: Bobbs-Merrill, 1971), p. 27-30.

4. Mark L. Knapp, *Nonverbal Communication in Human Interaction* (New York: Holt, Rinehart, & Winston, 1972), pp. 147-81.

5. Eisenberg and Smith, *Nonverbal Communication*, pp. 66-74.

6. The work of Ray Birdwhistell, in particular, and others, has demonstrated that there are various levels of kinesic study. For example, prekinesic study might determine the number of positions that an eyelid is capable of taking. Microkinesics has to do with determining which are discriminable and meaningful, and social kinesics investigates which have significance in social interaction. Similarly, with the development of language, there are innumerable sounds and combinations of sounds, but only certain ones actually are learned and used meaningfully. So we develop both linguistic abilities (formal symbol systems) and nonverbal abilities (informal symbol systems) that are finite and describable. Our acquisition of nonverbal skills thus is at least analogous to our development of language skills, our articulatory behaviors, word pronunciation, and semantic ability. See Eisenberg and Smith, *Nonverbal Communication*, p. 28.

7. Remark attributed to Andrew Wyeth by William Brower, in a presentation on the use of the voice in interpretative speech.

8. Conrad H. Massa, "Preaching as Confluence," *The Princeton Seminary Bulletin*, (September 1979), p. 110. Dr. Massa strongly asserts the identity between the sermon and the preacher: "The preacher is not merely one who 'delivers' the sermon; the preacher also *is* the sermon, the personification of this expression of faith."

9. Knapp, *Nonverbal Communication in Human Interaction*, p. 102.

10. I am indebted to W. J. Beeners for this concept of the "center" as the point of balance and motive force for gesture and movement in speech.

11. Knapp, *Nonverbal Communication in Human Interaction*, p. 121.

12. P. Ekman and W. V. Friesen, "Constants Across Cultures in the Face and Emotion," *Journal of Personality and Social Psychology*, vol. XVII (1971), pp. 124-29. Also, P. Ekman, "Universals and Cultural Differences in Facial Expressions of Emotion," J. Cole, ed., *Nebraska Symposium on Motivation*, 1971 (Lincoln: University of Nebraska Press, 1972). Cited in Knapp, *Nonverbal Communication in Human Interaction*, p. 129.

13. Eisenberg and Smith, *Nonverbal Communication*, pp. 96-97.

14. Bert Bradley, *Speech Performance* (Dubuque: Wm. C. Brown, 1967), p. 83.

15. Clyde E. Fant, *Preaching for Today* (New York: Harper & Row, 1975), p. 174.

16. Thich Nhat Hanh, "Our Green Garden," *Viet Nam Poems* (Santa Barbara: Unicorn Press, n.d.)

17. W. H. Auden, "In Memory of W. B. Yeats," *W. H. Auden: Collected Poems*, ed.

Edward Mendelson (New York: Random House, 1958), p. 53. © 1940 renewed 1968 by W. H. Auden.

CHAPTER VIII—THE PREACHING MOMENT REVISITED

1. Fant, *Preaching for Today*, pp. 112-26.
2. Dwight E. Stevenson and Charles F. Diehl, *Reaching People from the Pulpit* (New York: Harper & Brothers, 1958), p. 98.
3. An interesting treatment of the concept of meaning as inherent in a process of communication, rather than abstracted from it, can be found in Don Geiger, "Interpretation and the Locus of Poetic Meaning," Richard Hass and David A. Williams, eds., *The Study of Oral Interpretation* (Indianapolis: Bobbs-Merrill, 1975), pp. 150-65.
4. Critical methodology in speech communication is described in detail in Elton S. Carter and Iline Fife, "The Critical Approach," Clyde W. Dow, ed., *An Introduction to Graduate Study in Speech and Theatre* (East Lansing: Michigan State University Press, 1961), pp. 81-103.
5. Fosdick, "The Ideas That Use Us," *Riverside Sermons*.

INDEX